Italian warships slice through choppy seas
during maneuvers in the Bay of Naples.
Mussolini's highly vaunted fleet, reinforced
by German submarines and air power, waged a
three-year-long struggle with the Allies
for control of the strategic Mediterranean Sea.

THE MEDITERRANEAN

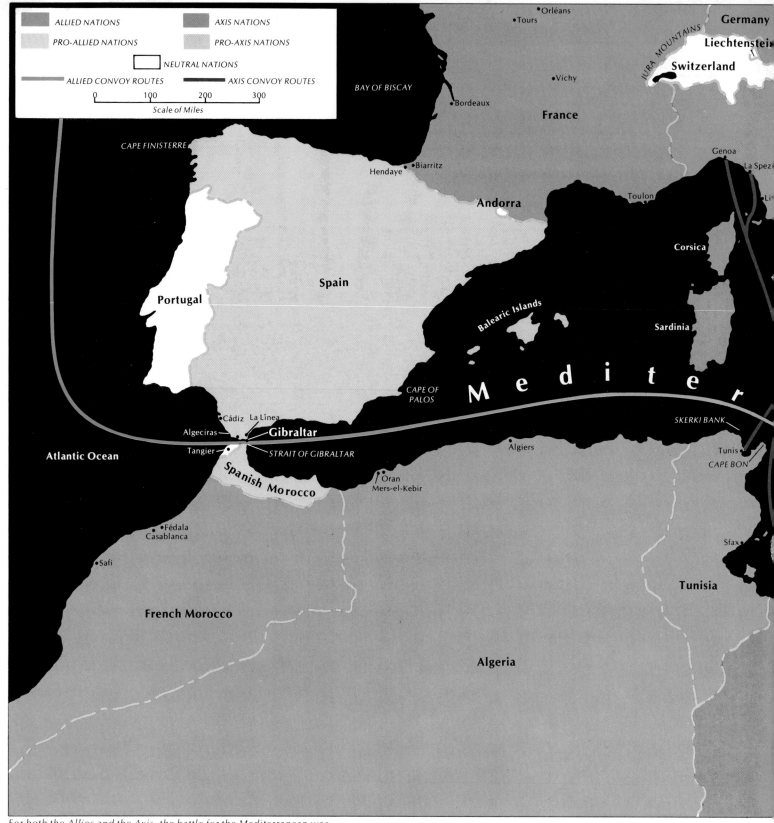

Legend

ALLIED NATIONS		AXIS NATIONS	
PRO-ALLIED NATIONS		PRO-AXIS NATIONS	
NEUTRAL NATIONS			
ALLIED CONVOY ROUTES		AXIS CONVOY ROUTES	

0   100   200   300
Scale of Miles

Orléans
Tours
Germany
JURA MOUNTAINS
Liechtenstein
Switzerland
Vichy

BAY OF BISCAY

Bordeaux

France

CAPE FINISTERRE

Genoa
La Spezia

Hendaye   Biarritz

Andorra

Toulon

Corsica

Spain

Balearic Islands

Sardinia

Portugal

CAPE OF
PALOS

M e d i t e r r

SKERKI BANK

Cádiz   La Línea

Algeciras   **Gibraltar**

Algiers

Tunis

Atlantic Ocean

Tangier   STRAIT OF GIBRALTAR

CAPE BON

Oran
Mers-el-Kebir

Spanish Morocco

Fédala
Casablanca

Sfax

Safi

Tunisia

French Morocco

Algeria

For both the Allies and the Axis, the battle for the Mediterranean was
from the outset a struggle to supply their own forces—and to deny
supplies to the enemy. To feed and reinforce its armies in Africa, the Axis
established a web of convoy routes (red lines) between Italian and
North African ports. Allied convoys (blue lines) entered the Mediterranean
at Gibraltar in the west and at the Suez Canal in the east; they supported
British forces based in Egypt and provisioned the tiny island of Malta,
a vital Allied outpost south of Sicily. The map also depicts, in the colors
indicated in the legend, the political alignment of the Mediterranean
countries as of the 10th of June, 1940—the day that Italy entered the War.

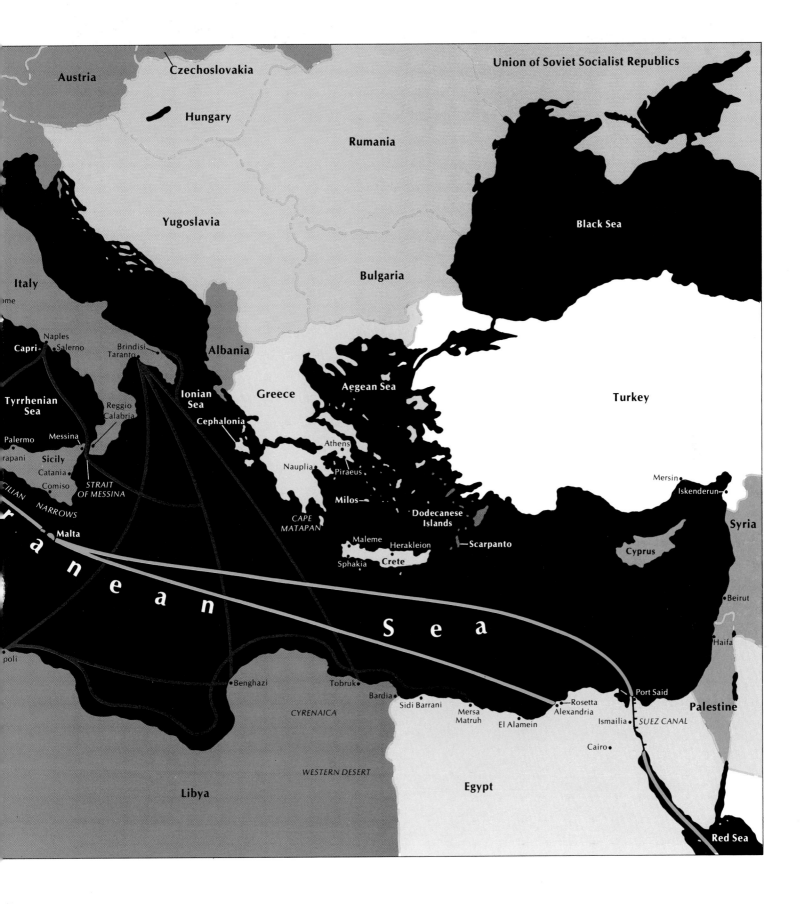

This volume is one of a series that chronicles
in full the events of the Second World War.
Previous books in the series include:

Prelude to War
Blitzkrieg
The Battle of Britain
The Rising Sun
The Battle of the Atlantic
Russia Besieged
The War in the Desert
The Home Front: U.S.A.
China-Burma-India
Island Fighting
The Italian Campaign
Partisans and Guerrillas
The Second Front
Liberation
Return to the Philippines
The Air War in Europe
The Resistance
The Battle of the Bulge
The Road to Tokyo
Red Army Resurgent
The Nazis
Across the Rhine
War under the Pacific
War in the Outposts
The Soviet Juggernaut
Japan at War

WORLD WAR II · TIME-LIFE BOOKS · ALEXANDRIA, VIRGINIA

BY A.B.C. WHIPPLE
AND THE EDITORS OF TIME-LIFE BOOKS

THE MEDITERRANEAN

Time-Life Books Inc.
is a wholly owned subsidiary of
TIME INCORPORATED

Founder: Henry R. Luce 1898-1967

Editor-in-Chief: Henry Anatole Grunwald
President: J. Richard Munro
Chairman of the Board: Ralph P. Davidson
Executive Vice President: Clifford J. Grum
Chairman, Executive Committee: James R. Shepley
Editorial Director: Ralph Graves
Group Vice President, Books: Joan D. Manley
Vice Chairman: Arthur Temple

TIME-LIFE BOOKS INC.

Managing Editor: Jerry Korn
Executive Editor: David Maness
Assistant Managing Editors: Dale M. Brown
(planning), George Constable, Martin Mann,
John Paul Porter, Gerry Schremp (acting)
Art Director: Tom Suzuki
Chief of Research: David L. Harrison
Director of Photography: Robert G. Mason
Assistant Art Director: Arnold C. Holeywell
Assistant Chief of Research: Carolyn L. Sackett
Assistant Director of Photography: Dolores A. Littles

Chairman: John D. McSweeney
President: Carl G. Jaeger
Executive Vice Presidents: John Steven Maxwell,
David J. Walsh
Vice Presidents: George Artandi (comptroller);
Stephen L. Bair (legal counsel); Peter G. Barnes;
Nicholas Benton (public relations); John L. Canova;
Beatrice T. Dobie (personnel); Carol Flaumenhaft
(consumer affairs); James L. Mercer (Europe/South
Pacific); Herbert Sorkin (production); Paul R. Stewart
(marketing)

WORLD WAR II

Editorial Staff for The Mediterranean
Editor: Gerald Simons
Designer/Picture Editor: Raymond Ripper
Chief Researcher: Charles S. Clark
Picture Editor: Clara Nicolai
Text Editors: Roger E. Herst, Robert Menaker,
Henry Woodhead
Staff Writers: Donald Davison Cantlay,
Richard D. Kovar, Brian McGinn
Researchers: Loretta Y. Britten, Kathleen Burke,
Gregory A. McGruder, Cronin Buck Sleeper,
Jayne T. Wise, Paula York
Art Assistant: Mikio Togashi
Editorial Assistant: Constance Strawbridge

Special Contributors
David S. Thomson (text), Jane Freundel Levey
(research)

Editorial Production
Production Editor: Feliciano Madrid
Operations Manager: Gennaro C. Esposito,
Gordon E. Buck (assistant)
Quality Control: Robert L. Young (director),
James J. Cox (assistant), Daniel J. McSweeney,
Michael G. Wight (associates)
Art Coordinator: Anne B. Landry
Copy Staff: Susan B. Galloway (chief), Allan Fallow,
Barbara F. Quarmby, Celia Beattie
Picture Department: Betty Hughes Weatherley
Traffic: Kimberly K. Lewis

Correspondents: Elisabeth Kraemer (Bonn); Margot
Hapgood, Dorothy Bacon, Lesley Coleman (London);
Susan Jonas, Lucy T. Voulgaris (New York); Maria
Vincenza Aloisi, Josephine du Brusle (Paris); Ann
Natanson (Rome). Valuable assistance was also
provided by Martha Mader (Bonn); Judy Aspinall,
Brian L. Davis, Jeremy Lawrence, Karin B. Pearce,
Pippa Pridham, Jill Rose, Pat Vaughn (London);
Godfrey Grima (Malta); Carolyn T. Chubet, Miriam
Hsia, Christina Lieberman (New York); Leonora
Dodsworth, Bianca Gabbrielli, Mimi Murphy (Rome).

The Author: A. B. C. WHIPPLE is a former assistant
managing editor of Time-Life Books. During World
War II he was Life's Pentagon correspondent, and
since then he has edited or collaborated on books
about Pearl Harbor and Douglas MacArthur. He also
has written numerous books on maritime history, four
of them for the Time-Life Books Seafarers series:
Fighting Sail, The Whalers, The Clipper Ships and The
Racing Yachts.

The Consultants: COLONEL JOHN R. ELTING, USA (Ret.),
is a military historian and author of The Battle of
Bunker's Hill, The Battles of Saratoga and Military
History and Atlas of the Napoleonic Wars. He edited
Military Uniforms in America: The Era of the Ameri-
can Revolution, 1755-1795 and Military Uniforms in
America: Years of Growth, 1796-1851, and was asso-
ciate editor of The West Point Atlas of American Wars.

HENRY H. ADAMS is a retired Navy captain who served
aboard the destroyer U.S.S. Owen in the major cam-
paigns of the central Pacific. After his service in World
War II he was a professor at the U.S. Naval Academy
in Annapolis, Maryland, and was later head of the
English Department at Illinois State University. His
books include 1942: The Year That Doomed the Axis,
Years of Deadly Peril, Years of Expectation, Years to
Victory and Harry Hopkins: A Biography.

DONALD MACINTYRE served with the Royal Navy during World War II as a commander of destroyers and
convoy escort groups in the North Atlantic. He was
awarded the Distinguished Service Order three times,
the Distinguished Service Cross and the American Le-
gion of Merit. Since his retirement in 1954 he has
written more than a score of books on naval historical
subjects, including U-Boat Killer, Narvik and Battle
for the Mediterranean.

Library of Congress Cataloguing in Publication Data

Whipple, Addison Beecher Colvin, 1918-
   The Mediterranean.

   (World War II; v. 27)
   Bibliography: p. 202
   Includes index.
   1. World War, 1939-1945—Mediterranean Sea.
2. World War, 1939-1945—Mediterranean region.
I. Time-Life Books.   II. Title.   III. Series.
D766.W47   940.54'21   80-29149
ISBN 0-8094-3385-0
ISBN 0-8094-3384-2 (lib. bdg.)
ISBN 0-8094-3383-4 (retail ed.)

For information about any Time-Life book, please write:

Reader Information
Time-Life Books
541 North Fairbanks Court
Chicago, Illinois 60611

CONTENTS

HITLER'S MOMENTOUS VISIT

On Italy's Mediterranean coast near Rome, Benito Mussolini, sniffing a rose, confers with a visiting Adolf Hitler and high-ranking officers in May 1938.

A SHOW OF UNITY BETWEEN DICTATORS

On May 2, 1938, after six months of staff work in Berlin, Adolf Hitler left the German capital for Italy, bringing with him on five special trains 500 Nazi Party officials, ranking military officers, SS bodyguards and reporters. It was a portentous visit: Hitler was eager to strengthen relations with his fellow dictator, Benito Mussolini, and to assure the Italians they had nothing to fear from the recent German takeover of neighboring Austria. Mussolini, nettled by Hitler's Austrian success, meant to reassert his leadership in the Axis by overawing the Führer with a display of Italy's might.

The centerpiece of Mussolini's martial show was to be a series of maneuvers in the Bay of Naples by the powerful Italian Navy. That fleet loomed large in the hopes of both nations. Mussolini intended to use it to forge a new Roman Empire around the rim of the Mediterranean. Hitler had no immediate designs on the Mediterranean basin, but it was clear that in the event of war the Italian fleet would be Germany's first line of defense in the south.

Hitler arrived in Rome on the evening of May 3, his train pulling into a brand new station built expressly to receive him. He was greeted effusively by Mussolini and coolly by Italy's anti-Nazi King, Victor Emmanuel III. Installed in the Royal Palace, Hitler briefly raised eyebrows by calling for "a woman"; it turned out that he wanted a chambermaid to turn down his bed.

The next day, the Duce ran the Führer ragged, and along with him his official photographers, Heinrich Hoffmann and Hugo Jaeger, many of whose pictures are published here for the first time. Hitler laid wreaths at Italy's Royal Tombs, the Tomb of the Unknown Soldier and the Fascist Altar. He lunched at the Palace, reviewed 50,000 Fascist youths, addressed German expatriates and rushed back to the Palace for a state dinner.

Worldly Romans were amused by the two dictators' pompous show of comradeship. When 2,600 trumpeters at the Fascist youth review sounded the "Wedding March" from *Lohengrin*—Hitler's favorite opera—more than one wit asked sarcastically, "Are they exchanging rings?"

On the first day of Hitler's visit, the Führer and the Duce stand at attention during a solemn ceremony in Rome at the Tomb of the Unknown Soldier.

At the rail of an Italian battleship, Hitler pensively awaits the beginning of the naval maneuvers that were to culminate his five-day-long visit to Italy.

DRESSING UP TO IMPRESS THE FÜHRER

Entraining from Rome late on May 4, Mussolini sped to Naples to ensure that all was in readiness for Hitler's reception and the Navy's maneuvers. In Naples, as in Rome and points between, public buildings and private homes had been decked with banners and signs welcoming the Führer. The fleet was ready: The last of 190 warships had arrived and the crews had finished putting their vessels in tiptop shape, both mechanically and cosmetically.

The fleet riding at anchor in the bay and tied up at Naples' docks was a handsome one. Its destroyers and cruisers were among the fastest and best-armed afloat, and its armada of nearly 100 submarines was—as the Duce boasted at every opportunity—the world's largest. Some Italian admirals complained that the Navy possessed no aircraft carriers, but Mussolini maintained that Italy itself was a giant aircraft carrier, that the land-based bombers of the Italian Air Force could easily interdict an enemy's shipping anywhere in the central Mediterranean.

In short, the Duce was well satisfied with his Navy. Little did he guess that Hitler was nearing Naples with a firm, adverse opinion of the Italian fleet. The Führer had been warned by German experts that three quarters of Italy's warships were obsolescent, and that because of a shortage of officers most of the submarines were commanded by petty officers.

Dressed with signal flags, the heavy cruiser Zara docks in Naples within sight of Mount Vesuvius.

Crewmen of the submarine fleet make their craft shipshape for maneuvers in Hitler's honor.

National flags, newly whitewashed buildings and signs stressing solidarity between the Axis powers enliven the view from Hitler's train as it rolls south.

NAPLES' GAUDY SALUTE OF WELCOME

Hitler's reception in Naples on the 5th of May was carefully orchestrated by the local Fascist Party. Neapolitans turned out to applaud the Führer as his motorcade wound past gaily festooned buildings and historic landmarks. But Hitler, who considered himself an authority on architecture, was unimpressed. "Naples," he later commented, "might be anywhere in South America."

Since most of the day was to be devoted to Mussolini's naval extravaganza, Hitler and his entourage hastened to the docks. There they were met by King Victor Emmanuel, and a launch ferried them to the flagship of the Italian Navy, the *Conte di Cavour*. On the deck of that battleship Mussolini greeted his Axis brother, and at a signal from the Duce the naval maneuvers got under way.

Residents of Naples welcome Adolf Hitler from balconies bedecked with Italian and Nazi flags.

Arriving for the naval show, the diminutive King Victor Emmanuel escorts Hitler and his party toward a saluting Army officer on the Naples waterfront.

Italian destroyers streak across the Bay of Naples at a full 38 knots while members of the ships' crews assemble along the rails in a salute to Hitler.

The 23,000-ton battleship *Conte di Cavour* (center) leads the parade of ships off Naples.

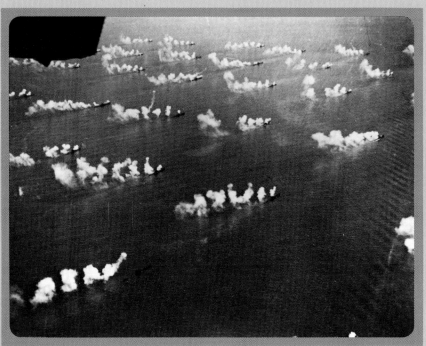

Puffs of smoke rise from 85 Italian submarines firing their deck guns simultaneously.

A DAZZLING DISPLAY BY THE DUCE'S FLEET

Gazing out over the Bay of Naples from the bridge of the battleship *Conte di Cavour*, Hitler witnessed a dazzling panoply of Italy's naval strength. On all sides, dozens of cruisers, destroyers and torpedo boats sliced in intricate patterns across the sunlit bay.

Reaching top speed, the warships began a dash out of the harbor. Just 25 minutes later—in one of the fastest naval getaways ever executed—the entire fleet had disappeared over the horizon.

The show continued in the clear blue waters off the island of Capri, where the cruisers *Fiume* and *Zara* put on a convincing demonstration of marksmanship. Gunners cranked up the cruisers' powerful 8-inch main batteries for maximum range and demolished a target ship anchored 11 miles distant.

Then Italy's underwater fleet stole the show. Eighty-five black-hulled submarines advanced toward the *Conte di Cavour* in nine columns, then dived simultaneously, disappearing beneath the waves in 75 seconds. Exactly eight minutes later, the submarines resurfaced, still in perfect formation, and their deck guns boomed out an 11-gun salute to the Führer, who seemed suitably impressed.

Even that tribute soon paled before the enormous homecoming spectacle Mussolini had contrived—at a cost of $340,000. As Naples' azure sky darkened, the hills surrounding the harbor blazed with electric lights that spelled out *Heil Hitler*.

At the end of the extravaganza put on by the Italian Navy at Naples, Hitler and Mussolini share a moment of jubilation with German Foreign Minister Joachim von Ribbentrop (far left), Italian Foreign Minister Count Galeazzo Ciano and Deputy Führer Rudolf Hess. "From now on," Mussolini vowed to Hitler, "no force will be able to separate us."

The 10,000-ton heavy cruiser Zara unleashes a salvo of shells from

her 8-inch guns in a final exhibition of marksmanship for the Führer. An aerial observer reported to the fleet: ''The salvo hit the target squarely.''

1

The early months of World War II were a frustrating time for Admiral Sir Andrew Browne Cunningham, Commander in Chief of Great Britain's Mediterranean fleet. He could attack neither the Germans nor their Italian allies; Hitler had no forces in the Mediterranean and Mussolini was observing the declaration of neutrality he had made at the outbreak of hostilities in September 1939. Cunningham could only wait and keep watch from his headquarters on Malta as Hitler's armies overran Poland and regrouped to attack in the West.

All this was maddening for a man of "A.B.C." Cunningham's disposition. He was a stubby bull terrier of a man, with a terrier's instinct for a fight. His zest for battle was matched by a lifelong love for the sea; as a child, when his professor-father asked him whether he would like to go into the Navy, he quickly replied, "Yes. I should like to be an admiral." Later, as a Naval cadet, he made frequent use of the traditional challenge "Fight you on Sunday"—with results that earned him the nickname "Meat Face." And as a young Naval officer he gravitated toward destroyers: They were the terriers of the Navy, always taking on bigger cruisers and battleships.

As a young lieutenant during World War I, Cunningham proved his scrappiness professionally, though not always in the approved manner. On one occasion he ignored his senior officer's recall order and took four destroyers charging after 13 German destroyers in the English Channel, returning only when the seas grew too rough for his guns to bear accurately. His foray was reported to the commodore of patrols, who shrugged it off as if to say, "That's Cunningham."

A gunnery officer assigned to serve under Cunningham between the Wars recalled that "He had a formidable reputation in the service as a martinet, and well-meaning friends condoled with me on what they told me I would be in for." But the gunnery officer found that although Cunningham's "most conspicuous quality was his intense spirit of attack, behind all his ferocity there was the kindest heart imaginable, laced with an almost boyish sense of humor." One who was less than comfortable with Cunningham's aggressiveness was a Royal Navy chaplain. One day Cunningham told him that his retirement dream was to "buy a house in an English village for the sheer joy of fighting the vicar." The chaplain promptly offered up a prayer: "Dear Lord, save me from being that vicar."

ROILING "CUNNINGHAM'S POND"

As he rose in rank, Cunningham became an adroit diplomat, moving smoothly through affairs of state and courtesy calls in foreign ports—none of which appealed to him as much as a brisk game of tennis. He was knighted early in 1939 after more than 40 years of distinguished service, 10 of them in his favorite Mediterranean waters; three months later, as war grew imminent, he was appointed Commander in Chief of Britain's extensive Mediterranean fleet.

Cunningham fully understood why Mussolini's first reaction was to declare Italy neutral despite his imperial ambitions and his treaty of alliance with Hitler. Approximately 80 per cent of Italy's imported goods came by sea, and the British, controlling the two gateways to the Mediterranean at Gibraltar and the Suez Canal, would move automatically to cut off these imports in the event of war. Moreover, except for Italy and Italian Libya, the entire Mediterranean basin was either Allied or neutral—and it was likely to remain so. The Italians did have a large and formidable Navy, but it was outweighed by the combined Mediterranean fleets of Britain and France. The Mediterranean seemed indeed to be what British journalists had begun to call it: "Cunningham's Pond."

The balance of power began to change, however, before a shot was fired in the Mediterranean. Between March and June of 1940, the Wehrmacht swept into Denmark, Norway, the Netherlands, Luxembourg, Belgium and France. Cunningham was required to lend several of his important vessels—including his own flagship, the battleship *Warspite*—to fight in the Battle of the Atlantic. To make up for Cunningham's reduced strength, the French sent a squadron of warships to Alexandria, Egypt's major port. The French also assumed increased responsibility for the western Mediterranean, with help from the Gibraltar-based Force H, a British Naval unit that operated in the Atlantic as well as in the Mediterranean.

Allied naval superiority in the Mediterranean had suddenly been spread thin. It was only a matter of time, Cunningham felt, before German successes in the north would tempt the "hyena"—as he customarily referred to Mussolini—to come in "to share the carcass." Prompted by warlike noises from Italy, Cunningham in May moved his warships to Alexandria from his precarious island headquarters on Malta, just 70-odd miles from Italian bomber bases in Sicily.

And the British Admiralty began returning the warships borrowed from the Mediterranean fleet.

On the 10th of June, 1940, Mussolini took the plunge, declaring war on Great Britain and France. Cunningham finally had his fight.

It had been anticipated all along that war would again engulf the ancient wellspring of Western civilization, with its historic and still-crucial trade routes. Neither side could hold Europe securely so long as the Continent's southern flank was exposed to attack from the Mediterranean. The temperate sea was a main artery of worldwide communication, and the mere fact of Italy's declaration of war closed it to all but the most urgent of Allied convoys, forcing most ships to take the safer, 12,000-mile route around the continent of Africa. Axis convoys from Italy had to provision and reinforce their armies in North Africa. To Britain, whose Empire depended on access to the countries bordering and beyond the Mediterranean, especially the oil-rich Middle East, the sea was a battleground of supreme importance. The winning of the Mediterranean would not win the War, but it would enable land armies to win the War.

The long, narrow configuration of the Mediterranean (Europe and Africa are nowhere more than 850 miles apart) made for a special kind of combat—one in which ships were more frequently opposed by land-based aircraft than by enemy ships. The Germans and later the British and Americans perfected the art of dive bombing a moving vessel. The dawn of the dive bomber signaled the decline of the dreadnought as the chief naval weapon, and it was in the Mediterranean that the battleship was first rivaled by the aircraft carrier. The Mediterranean war also confirmed the deadly efficacy of the low-altitude torpedo bomber: In a single, devastating attack, a handful of these planes crippled the Italian fleet and provided a pattern for the Japanese assault a year later on the United States fleet at Pearl Harbor.

The Mediterranean war furnished an early testing ground for newly developed arms—radar, torpedo boats, torpedoes with magnetic detonating devices. The Mediterranean war saw history's biggest assault force—larger by two divisions than the one that eventually landed in Normandy—put ashore on Sicily. Not least, the Mediterranean war brought to the fore many of the War's ablest commanders.

The struggle to control the Mediterranean would ebb and flow for three years. It was, of course, a struggle quite unlike the great battles on land. The sailors had to endure long periods of tense, watchful waiting on board relatively comfortable ships, a regimen broken only periodically by outbursts of fierce combat. There were other anomalies to the Mediterranean war, but none were as strange as the first great clash of the campaign, in July of 1940. It was a battle not between enemies but between erstwhile partners: the Royal Navy and a fleet of its fallen French allies.

There was no sign of trouble between the British and the French on June 10, the day that Italy declared war. But there were signs of terrible disarray in the Allied camp. The French government abandoned Paris just four days before advancing German armies occupied the capital. The French bureaucrats fled south to Orléans, west to Tours, south to Bordeaux and finally northeast to Vichy, their new seat of government. During this period the various units of the French Navy were often out of contact with their peripatetic commander, Admiral of the Fleet Jean François Darlan. If communication had not been broken, a bloody clash between comrades might have been avoided.

At 1 p.m. on June 11, less than 24 hours after Cunningham received word of Italy's declaration of war, he eagerly took the British Mediterranean fleet to sea—and to more frustration. The warships on the move made an impressive spectacle, their gray hulls slicing through the water, their white-uniformed crews striking mooring lines. The battleships *Malaya* and *Warspite* (which had returned a month earlier from duty in the Atlantic) and the aircraft carrier *Eagle* steamed grandly past the breakwater protecting Alexandria harbor and into the open Mediterranean. At the *Warspite's* masthead, snapping in the breeze, was the admiral's flag, the red Saint George's Cross on a field of white. Off the harbor entrance the capital ships were joined by their shepherding force of nine destroyers and two cruisers.

Planes from the *Eagle* swept ahead in circles, searching for elements of the Italian fleet. They found nothing by evening, and swung south toward the North African coast on the second leg of a triangular sweep. In the dark of night came the first sign of the enemy—an explosion. An Italian submarine had approached undetected and sent a torpedo into the hull of the cruiser *Calypso*. It was a fatal hit. Destroyers hurried alongside; life rafts plopped into the black water and ships' boats rushed in among the bobbing heads of the *Calypso's* men, who had abandoned ship. All but 39 of them were rescued, but the holed cruiser sank in an hour and a half. First blood had been claimed by the Axis, and despite further evidence of enemy submarines, Cunningham returned to Alexandria empty-handed.

While Cunningham was making his sweep of the eastern Mediterranean, the French squadron based at Alexandria made a similar circuit of the Aegean, returning to port with the same lack of success. The commander of the French squadron was Vice Admiral René Godfroy, who had become a close friend of Cunningham's. Godfroy, depressed by the defeats suffered by the French Army, had welcomed the opportunity to join the British in attacking the Italian Navy, if they could find it. Undeterred by their vain excursions, Godfroy and Cunningham decided to make their next search farther west, in the central Mediterranean.

June 11 brought much greater discouragement to the Allied governments. Prime Minister Winston Churchill flew to a town near Orléans for consultation with Britain's faltering, retreating ally. In what he characterized as a "miserable discussion," it became clear that France would shortly have to sue for a separate peace even though its government had pledged never to do so. Churchill reiterated his determination that Britain would fight on alone, but the French leader-

Admiral Sir Andrew Browne Cunningham stands jauntily at the rail of his flagship, the Warspite. Cunningham's combative leadership as the commander of Britain's Mediterranean fleet caused his Navy colleagues to compare him with the legendary Horatio Lord Nelson.

As Adolf Hitler looks on, Count Galeazzo Ciano (seated, left) and Joachim von Ribbentrop sign the Pact of Steel on May 22, 1939. The Italians, unprepared for war, believed German assurances that the alliance would daunt France and Britain and assure at least three more years of peace.

ship believed that Britain too would soon succumb, and that France must learn to live in a world dominated by Germany. Before he left for home, Churchill singled out Admiral Darlan—"this ambitious, self-seeking and capable admiral," he called him—for a special appeal. Darlan had been responsible for building the French Navy into a formidable force in a long arms race with Italy's Navy. "Darlan, you must never let them get the French fleet," Churchill warned. Darlan promised that the French Navy would never surrender to the Germans.

True to Darlan's word, most of the Naval vessels in French ports later sailed to harbors of at least temporary refuge. Two battleships, four cruisers and eight destroyers put into the British harbors of Plymouth and Portsmouth. Two unfinished battleships, the *Jean Bart* and the *Richelieu*, fled south to Casablanca and Dakar respectively. Besides Godfroy's squadron in Alexandria, there remained a powerful force in Mers-el-Kebir, a few miles west of the French Algerian city of Oran, and a number of small Naval units in French territories in the Western Hemisphere. It was by no means certain what these scattered forces would do in the event of a French capitulation.

As Churchill feared, the collapse of France was soon complete. On June 22 the French government signed an armistice with Germany. It established the German occupation of northern France while guaranteeing a "neutral" southern France under the cooperative administration of oc-

togenarian Marshal Henri Philippe Pétain. On the crucial disposition of the French Navy, the armistice terms offered encouraging assurances:

"The French war fleet, with the exception of those units released to the French government for protection of French interests in the colonial empire, is to assemble in ports to be later designated, and is there to be demobilized and disarmed under the control of Germany and Italy.

The German government solemnly declares to the French government that it does not intend to use for its own ends during the War the French war fleet stationed in the harbors under German control, with the exception of units necessary for guarding the coasts and for minesweeping."

Although the precise terms of the armistice were not yet known in London, Churchill was by no means confident that the Axis leaders could resist appropriating whatever French warships came into their grasp. Certainly Hitler and Mussolini could not be trusted. Could Darlan? Churchill thought not. Darlan's great-grandfather had been killed in the Battle of Trafalgar, Churchill recalled. He regarded the chief of the French Navy as "one of those good Frenchmen who hate England."

The War Cabinet discussions that ensued in London were painful. Churchill was convinced that if the French Navy, the fourth largest in the world, were merged with the enemy's forces, the balance of power in the Mediterranean would swing to the Axis; even worse, the increased naval

strength might assure the success of Hitler's threatened invasion of England. Unless the commanders of the French fleet could be persuaded to steam out and join the Royal Navy, Churchill could see no alternative to its neutralization—by any means necessary.

At first the British Prime Minister was opposed by most of his military advisers, who repeated German and Italian statements that they had no intention of employing French vessels except for coastal protection and minesweeping. Churchill's aides argued that no French Naval officer would permit his ship to be used against France's recent allies.

In this dispute Churchill had one major ally: President Franklin D. Roosevelt. The United States was not then in the War, but its British sympathies were no secret and it was supporting Britain's war effort in every way a noncombatant could. The American Ambassador to France, William C. Bullitt, had persuaded Roosevelt that the French leaders' "physical and moral defeat has been so absolute that they have accepted completely for France the fate of becoming a province of Nazi Germany." The American Army's chief of staff, General George C. Marshall, and Chief of Naval Operations Admiral Harold R. Stark were so concerned at the

prospect that Axis naval forces operating in the Atlantic might be augmented by the French fleet that they were proposing a shift of the major part of the U.S. fleet to the Atlantic from its base at Pearl Harbor.

On June 27 the War Cabinet agreed on what Churchill himself called "a hateful decision, the most unnatural and painful in which I have ever been concerned." The French admirals must be given an ultimatum: At the very least they must neutralize their fleet—or lose their ships.

An intricate set of maneuvers, code-named Operation *Catapult,* was quickly mounted to confront the major elements of the French fleet simultaneously and by surprise. The primary target was the strong force in Mers-el-Kebir, whose major vessels were two battleships and the formidable new battle cruisers *Dunkerque* and *Strasbourg,* each mounting eight 13-inch guns and capable of nearly 30 knots. This force, which also included six destroyers and a seaplane carrier, was under the command of Vice Admiral Marcel Bruno Gensoul.

On June 28, Vice Admiral Sir James Somerville was ordered to take command of the Gibraltar-based Force H—at that time consisting chiefly of two battleships, the battle

cruiser *Hood*, the carrier *Ark Royal*, two cruisers and 11 destroyers—and to steam for Mers-el-Kebir.

A day later the first word of the operation reached Cunningham in Alexandria. His response was immediate and strong disapproval. "To me," he wrote, "the idea was utterly repugnant." Launching hostilities against their allies seemed to him "an act of sheer treachery" and "almost inept in its unwisdom." Furthermore, he protested to the Admiralty, "it was unthinkable that Admiral Darlan, who had spent all his life and energy in building up the fleet, would tamely deliver it to the enemy." Cunningham concluded that Operation *Catapult* would turn every Frenchman against Britain, that the French fleet would resist with determination, and that the Royal Navy, already stretched to the limit, might be crippled in such an action.

Cunningham's protests were echoed from Gibraltar. On arrival there, Somerville had conferred with experts on the French fleet. They too were appalled. Admiral Sir Dudley North, Britain's flag officer for the North Atlantic, had only a few days earlier talked with Gensoul in Mers-el-Kebir: The French admiral had fervently promised that he would never let his ships be commandeered by the Axis. North's views were supported by Captain Cedric S. Holland, formerly British Naval attaché in Paris, who knew and trusted Gensoul as a friend. At least two other senior British officers also argued against such precipitate action. Somerville summed up this advice in a message to the Admiralty, proposing that at least diplomacy should be tried before resorting to attack. No self-respecting French Naval officer, everyone agreed, could respond to the proposed British ultimatum except with strong resistance. Somerville had a countersuggestion; send French-speaking Captain Holland ahead to see if he could persuade his friend Gensoul to bring his ships out to join the British.

But Somerville and Cunningham were too late. No one in the War Cabinet was prepared to reopen the unpleasant discussion. Nevertheless Churchill dispatched a sympathetic message to Somerville: "You are charged with one of the most disagreeable and difficult tasks that a British admiral has ever been faced with." A partial compromise was reached. Captain Holland could present the British demands to the French, but only with Admiral Somerville's squadron in readiness on the scene, and the demands still

amounted unmistakably to an ultimatum. The four alternatives offered to Gensoul were:

(1) Bring out his fleet to join the Royal Navy.
(2) Take his fleet to a British port with reduced crews, which would be repatriated.
(3) Sail to a French West Indian or U.S. port and decommission the fleet there.
(4) Scuttle the ships where they were in Mers-el-Kebir harbor.

If Gensoul would not accept any of these options, Somerville's instructions were explicit: Sink the French fleet, especially the battle cruisers *Dunkerque* and *Strasbourg*.

Meanwhile, Admiral Gensoul and the other French Naval commanders had received definitive orders from Admiral Darlan. In announcing the armistice, Darlan said: "Demobilized warships must remain French with French flags, reduced French crews, stationed in French metropolitan or colonial ports. Secret preparations for sabotage will be made so that no enemy or foreigner seizing a ship by force will be able to make use of it." Two days later, Darlan warned his officers that "to answer interested appeals from

Italians throng the Piazza Venezia in Rome on the 10th of June, 1940, to hear Mussolini's declaration of war. Placards extol the Duce, the King and Italian might in the Mediterranean, or Mare Nostrum (Our Sea).

The crew of an Italian minelayer prepares to sow a field of bulbous contact mines in the Sicilian Narrows. Four days before declaring war, Italy warned that its coasts already were dangerous to navigation.

SUEZ: THE MEDITERRANEAN'S VULNERABLE BACK DOOR

On the lookout for Axis bombers, a trio of high-winged RAF Westland Lysanders, noted for the good visibility they afforded pilot and crew, patrols the vulnerable Suez Canal.

Heavy losses among convoys that ventured into the western Mediterranean via Gibraltar early in the War forced the Allies to turn to a slower but safer alternate route to the Middle East: the 12,000-mile run around the continent of Africa, up the Red Sea and through the Suez Canal.

The 100-mile-long canal, engineered by the Frenchman Ferdinand de Lesseps and opened in 1869, was the vital link to the eastern Mediterranean and the lands beyond. Admiral Cunningham called it "our back door"; he knew that if the door was shut, Britain's forces in Egypt might wither and collapse for lack of supplies.

The canal's importance was not lost on the Axis. On January 30, 1941, Luftwaffe planes based on Rhodes struck the Suez in force, roaring in at tree level to drop magnetic mines into the narrow, shallow waterway. The mines soon claimed a number of ships, whose hulks clogged the canal for days at a time.

At its northern end, the Suez Canal opens into the sea (right) at Port Said, an Egyptian city near the eastern tip of the Mediterranean.

The British could spare very few planes from the battlefronts to intercept the German raiders, so they responded with what forces they had. British, Indian and Egyptian troops ranged the length of the canal to pour concentrated small-arms fire on the intruding aircraft, and sentries stationed along the banks spotted and recorded the fall of mines. In the meantime, Red Sea port facilities were expanded so that more cargo could be transshipped by road and rail to Alexandria, avoiding the Suez bottleneck.

In time, the canal was saved for Allied use by Germany's preoccupations elsewhere. Hitler gradually moved Luftwaffe squadrons from the Mediterranean to support Operation *Barbarossa*, his invasion of the Soviet Union. The remaining German warplanes were diverted to other pressing objectives: interdicting the Mediterranean fleet and supporting the Afrika Korps. The Suez again became a clear funnel through which Allied ships, men and supplies poured into the Mediterranean.

abroad would result in our metropolitan territory becoming a German province."

It was July 2 before the exchanges between Gibraltar and London concluded and Somerville received his final instructions. That evening Force H moved out of Gibraltar's harbor and steamed southeast; Captain Holland was in the van on the destroyer *Foxhound*. By dawn on July 3 the coast of North Africa was in view. At 6:20 a.m. the *Foxhound* reached the entrance to Mers-el-Kebir harbor, where Holland directed this message to the French flagship: "The British Admiralty has sent Captain Holland to confer with you. The British Navy hopes their proposal will enable you and your glorious French Navy to range yourself side by side with them. In these circumstances your ships would remain yours and no one need have any anxiety for the future." The flattery and the reassurances were capped by an ominous euphemism: "A British fleet is at sea off Oran waiting to welcome you." Later a similar message was broadcast directly to several French warships so that Britain's offer could not be withheld from them by their commanders.

For an hour and a half, the *Foxhound* sat off the breakwater, rolling gently in the Mediterranean swells, while the sun rose to reveal the formidable shapes of the French battleships and battle cruisers lying side by side in the harbor, across from a row of destroyers. Then a small craft set out from the flagship *Dunkerque,* closest to the shore. It was the admiral's barge, and as it came alongside the *Foxhound,* Gensoul's flag lieutenant presented the admiral's response: Gensoul was too busy to see Holland but would send his chief of staff. Holland was adamant—his business was with

Gensoul, and Gensoul alone. The flag lieutenant saluted, the barge's engine sputtered to life again and the little craft headed back into the harbor bearing Holland's message. Soon after, the French signaled the *Foxhound* to depart; Gensoul did not want to negotiate.

Holland would not give up so easily. Ordering a motor launch over the side, he climbed down into it and headed toward the harbor. Gensoul's flag lieutenant met Holland at the harbor entrance and once more announced that Admiral Gensoul would not receive his visitor. With no other choice, Holland gave the flag lieutenant the ultimatum he had brought for Gensoul. It was written in French and in English, and it presented in language as politely diplomatic as possible the reason for the terms the British Admiralty had insisted upon: "His Majesty's government finds it impossible from their previous experience to believe that Germany and Italy will not at any moment which suits them seize French warships and use them against Britain." If Admiral Gensoul would not join the British, or surrender or scuttle the ships under his command, "I have the orders of His Majesty's government to use whatever force may be necessary to prevent your ships from falling into German or Italian hands."

Gensoul tried in vain to report his predicament to Admiral Darlan, who was then in transit between Bordeaux and Vichy; Darlan heard nothing of the confrontation until it was too late. But Gensoul got through to the French Admiralty, and said that a British force had offered him a choice of scuttling his ships or seeing them sunk by naval gunfire. For some reason, Gensoul said nothing about the other, less

Commander of the French Navy Admiral Jean François Darlan (right) rides with Marshal Henri Philippe Pétain, who became head of the Vichy government. Darlan promised Britain's Prime Minister Churchill that the French Navy would never serve Germany.

extreme options offered him, and the outraged French officials issued a call to arms: All French Naval forces in the Mediterranean were to prepare for battle.

Captain Holland had meanwhile been waiting on board the motor launch at the harbor entrance, still hoping for a chance to board the *Dunkerque* and use whatever influence he still had with Gensoul. A further appeal had brought another negative response from Gensoul, who sent Holland a defiant note: "The assurances given by Admiral Gensoul to Admiral Sir Dudley North remain the same. French warships will meet force by force." Signs of preparing for action became noticeable on the French vessels. Awnings were being furled and smoke was rising from the funnels, as if the French were getting ready to steam out to battle. Somerville, warned of this activity, relayed the news to London, where the First Sea Lord, Admiral Sir Dudley Pound, suggested mining the harbor to keep the French warships trapped inside. Shortly after 1 p.m. a flight of planes from the *Ark Royal* swooped down and dropped mines across the harbor's mouth. No French planes were available to challenge them.

Finally, Holland received word that Gensoul would see him. He raced into the harbor and at 4:15 p.m. climbed the *Dunkerque's* gangway. His old friend greeted him stiffly. Gensoul announced again that he would never surrender his fleet to the Germans or Italians. But neither could he in honor surrender to an ultimatum from the British, especially—and this obviously had enraged him—when they had committed the hostile act of mining his harbor entrance, thereby making it impossible for him to proceed to sea and accept any of the first three options. His implication was that these alternatives had been offered in bad faith.

At 4:46, while Holland was reasoning with Gensoul, Somerville received a warning from the Admiralty: "Settle matters quickly or you will have reinforcements to deal with." At 5:15 p.m.—1715 military time—Somerville signaled the *Dunkerque:* "If none of the British proposals are acceptable by 1730, it will be necessary to sink your ships."

Captain Holland had failed, and he would have to run for his life. As he stepped onto the *Dunkerque's* gangway at 5:25 p.m., just five minutes before the deadline, "Action Stations" sounded aboard all the French warships. Holland raced for the entrance to the harbor. In his last close-up look at the French fleet he saw the officer of the watch on board the *Bretagne* saluting him smartly as his launch swept past the battleship.

Holland had scarcely passed the breakwater when the British fleet opened fire. The first salvo came from Somerville's flagship, the battle cruiser *Hood*. Her 15-inch shells smashed into the *Bretagne*, which threw a tower of flame into the late-afternoon sky. Then the British force fired at will, its big guns scoring a number of fiery hits. A dense black cloud spread behind Holland as he raced away from the harbor to safety.

Mers-el-Kebir nearly disappeared in a caldron of flame and greasy smoke. The destroyer *Mogador* could be seen settling into the water, her stern blown off by one of Somerville's 15-inch shells. The battleship *Provence*, her guns answering, moved across the harbor before erupting in an explosion and running aground on the beach. The flagship *Dunkerque* fired off 40 rounds at the *Hood*, but all of them missed, and shortly the *Dunkerque's* guns too fell silent. In less than a quarter of an hour the harbor had become a smoldering tangle of blackened metal.

Gensoul signaled for a cease-fire. Somerville complied, but added, "Unless I see your ships sinking I shall open fire again." Then, to save any accidental loss of British lives as the French were blowing up their ships, he took his fleet out of range, confident that the mines at the harbor entrance would prevent the French from getting away.

But one French vessel, the battle cruiser *Strasbourg,* had begun a daring move to escape. In a superb feat of seamanship, and aided by the concealing smoke, her captain took his ship through the wreckage littering the harbor, picked his way safely through the minefield and was running for the open sea before Somerville's ships had circled back onto the scene. The *Strasbourg* was nearly out of danger when one of the *Ark Royal's* pilots spotted her. Somerville sent six torpedo planes in pursuit, but they were unable to stop the French battle cruiser. Somerville chased her for a while in the *Hood,* but then let her go rather than leave the harbor entrance uncovered again, and the *Strasbourg* steamed safely into Toulon harbor the next evening.

However, the *Dunkerque,* the *Bretagne,* the *Provence* and the *Mogador* were beyond escape. They lay crippled or beached in the harbor of Mers-el-Kebir. More than 1,200

Frenchmen, who less than a month earlier had been fighting alongside the British, had died under the guns of their former allies. The British had lost not a man.

In Alexandria, meanwhile, Cunningham had been ordered to present virtually the same ultimatum to his friend Admiral Godfroy, and he sent him a formal invitation to meet on board the *Warspite* at 7 a.m. on July 3. It was "an unusual hour," Cunningham admitted, "which must have caused him to realize that something momentous was about to happen." Godfroy was punctual. He was piped aboard and greeted by a Royal Marine band. With their aides, the two admirals settled down in armchairs in Cunningham's cabin. Their conversation was formal: They spoke in English, with the British officers stressing an occasional important point in French. Cunningham described the Admiralty's proposals, adding that the decision must be made that day. Godfroy was cordial, though his friend could detect the strain behind his calm exterior.

Cunningham presented three options. The first was to integrate the French vessels into the British fleet "so that they can continue the struggle against the enemy side by side with the British Navy." This course of action appeared unacceptable to Godfroy; he had no desire to have his government condemn his sailors as deserters or traitors for fighting under the British flag. Godfroy also believed that if he handed over his squadron to the British, the Germans might well occupy southern France as a punitive measure, as Admiral Darlan had warned.

The second proposal—that Admiral Godfroy immobilize his ships—seemed more palatable. Cunningham promised that in such a case the British would assume responsibility for the pay and provisioning of the French crews. Certainly the third option was considerably less attractive: Take the French fleet to sea and scuttle it. "This," Cunningham recorded dryly, "evoked no enthusiasm."

Godfroy asked for time to make a decision. Cunningham suggested a deadline of 1 p.m. Godfroy replied, "Oh, sooner than that," and 11:30 a.m. was agreed upon. The meeting recessed. Godfroy and his chief of staff climbed down into the admiral's barge and rode back to his flagship, the cruiser *Duquesne*.

It was an anxious wait for Cunningham, who knew that while Godfroy was making his decision, Somerville was presenting the Admiralty's ultimatum to Gensoul more than 2,000 miles to the west. If something went wrong at Mersel-Kebir and word of it reached Godfroy, he might renounce his inclination to neutralize his squadron. He might

even conclude that he had no choice but to resist the British by force of arms.

Godfroy's answer came by letter in French at noon, and it was, Cunningham wrote, "a bitter disappointment." On reflection, Godfroy had decided that he could neither permit his ships to join the Royal Navy nor disarm them in a foreign port without authorization from Vichy—and that would take time. He therefore reluctantly accepted the third option: He would proceed to sea and scuttle his squadron. But for such an operation he would need 48 hours to prepare.

Cunningham was now in a quandary. He realized that Godfroy might be stalling. But no good officer could easily commit himself to a course of action in open violation of his orders, and there was little question that Godfroy would need more time than the few hours remaining of July 3 to prepare his fleet for scuttling. Still, Cunningham understood the Admiralty's sense of urgency and the tricky relationship between events at Alexandria and at Mers-el-Kebir.

At this point Cunningham, the veteran of 43 years' service, decided to take a chance. During the early stages of negotiation he had meticulously followed London's instructions. Now, despite the Admiralty's orders to disarm the French squadron before the day was out, he agreed to Godfroy's request for a delay of 48 hours. Responding to his friend's letter with a formal letter of his own, Cunningham explained that his instructions left him "no alternative but to accept your choice" of scuttling the French squadron. "I am therefore under the painful necessity," he wrote, "of asking you to proceed to sea to carry out your purpose at 1200 on Friday, 5th July." He reported this decision to the Admiralty. But he also wrote a second letter to Godfroy—one that he kept from his superiors in defiance of specific orders.

It was a plea from one friend to another. Could Godfroy make some sort of gesture that would prove to the British government he did not intend to attempt an escape to sea? If, for example, he would discharge his fuel and take the warheads off his torpedoes, the Admiralty might be convinced that Godfroy had no intention of fleeing from Alexandria with his fleet.

Godfroy agreed almost at once. By 5:30 p.m. French tankers had begun draining fuel from the warships, indicating that Godfroy was as good as his word. Cunningham sighed with relief, and informed the Admiralty that the crisis seemed over. The French squadron would stay in Alexandria. How to dispose of the ships remained to be decided, but at least the tension that had been building all day was relieved. So Cunningham, relaxing for the first time in 24 hours, was unprepared for the double blow that followed.

In the early summer of 1940, British and French warships ride at their moorings in the harbor at Alexandria. On July 4, Admiral Cunningham undertook delicate negotiations for the disarmament of the French vessels.

The first came by radio from London, at 8:15 p.m.: ADMIRALTY NOTE THAT OIL FUEL IS BEING DISCHARGED BY FRENCH SHIPS. REDUCTION OF CREWS, ESPECIALLY BY RATINGS, SHOULD HOWEVER BEGIN AT ONCE BY LANDING OR TRANSFER TO MERCHANT SHIPS, BEFORE DARK TONIGHT. DO NOT, REPEAT NOT, FAIL. This peremptory order, Cunningham wrote later, "filled me with indignation. It showed no comprehension whatever of the explosive atmosphere at Alexandria or the difficult conditions in which we were working." Even more ridiculous, the message demanding compliance before dark was sent from London after sunset Alexandria time. Cunningham guessed that the order had come from some ignorant Navy bureaucrat and decided to ignore it. Then the second blow fell.

Cunningham had scarcely finished reading the dispatch from London when he was handed a formal letter in French from Godfroy. Under the stiff salutation of "Admiral," Godfroy wrote that he had learned of the Royal Navy's ultimatum to Gensoul at Mers-el-Kebir. The French Admiralty had ordered Godfroy to take his fleet to sea. He was stalling by asking for confirmation of the order. But in the meantime he had halted the discharge of fuel.

More exchanges went back and forth between the *Warspite* and the *Duquesne* throughout the evening of July 3. Godfroy explained coldly but courteously that his new orders had removed the option of scuttling his fleet at sea. If he left the harbor, he was bound to attempt an escape. He had, however, made a promise and would keep it. If directly ordered to do so by the Royal Navy, he would scuttle the squadron under Cunningham's guns. He would, he added with Gallic nicety, try to sink his ships in such a way as to block the harbor as little as possible.

By then it was midnight. Cunningham described the new situation to London, reported that he intended to order the scuttling next morning, and climbed into bed for an exhausted sleep. He was awakened before 7 a.m. on July 4 with the news of an even greater crisis. An aide brought an angry message from Godfroy, who had learned after midnight that Somerville's Force H had fired on the French fleet at Mers-el-Kebir. Because of this attack, Godfroy repudiated all his promises, claiming he had made them to an officer who was dealing in bad faith. Godfroy intended to head for the open sea, fighting his way out if necessary.

Cunningham hurried on deck. Steam was already being raised in the French vessels. Their guns were being readied for action. "The crisis had come," Cunningham wrote later. "There now seemed to be no chance of evading what I wished at all costs to avoid, a battle in Alexandria harbor."

Orders went crackling through the British fleet. The battleships maneuvered to bring their broadsides to bear on the French ships. Tampions came out of the muzzles of the guns. Submarine and destroyer commanders were directed to put to sea, and prepare to torpedo or shell any French vessel that got out of the harbor or opened fire. Then Cunningham tried a last, desperate gamble.

There remained, he calculated, a few hours before the French ships could raise enough steam pressure in their boilers to move out under their own power; at least the marathon negotiations had kept the French from firing up their boilers before now. Summoning his staff, Cunningham laid out his plan. Clearly Admiral Godfroy felt that his honor left him no choice but to fight. He needed an excuse not to. The British would provide that excuse by going over Godfroy's head to his officers and men and spurring them to peaceful rebellion. "It was a most distasteful task," Cunningham recalled, "but the only possible thing to do."

N'oubliez pas Oran!

A German propaganda poster bearing the legend "Remember Oran!" depicts a drowning French sailor clutching a Tricolor. Posters such as this were employed to inflame anti-British sentiment, born of the Royal Navy's preemptive attack on the French fleet at Mers-el-Kebir, near Oran.

Immediately a message was prepared in French, addressed to everyone in the squadron. "In it," Cunningham explained, "we set out the helplessness of their situation; our sincere desire not to fight with or kill any of them if they tried to get away; and the generous terms the British government offered, which we assured them could be accepted without loss of dignity or honor."

The message was flashed in French to every ship in the French fleet. It was also written on large blackboards that were carried by ships' boats through the harbor. And Cunningham ordered another ploy, directed especially at Godfroy's officers. Throughout the time the French had been moored in Alexandria harbor, one of Cunningham's officers had been assigned to each French vessel as an unofficial host. This gesture of courtesy now provided a serendipitous reward: Each British host went aboard his appointed French ship to reason with the friends he had made during their months as allies.

Through the critical hours of the morning, Cunningham stood on the bridge studying the decks of the French squadron through his binoculars. His message had brought no response. But he could see groups of sailors gathering in heated discussion, and one by one his host officers returned to report an almost unanimously cordial reception. One French commander had already made his decision: He told his British host, "When I saw the tampions being removed from your guns, I immediately ordered the tampions to be placed in mine."

Cunningham watched in suspense as all the French captains, obviously summoned by Godfroy, went aboard the flagship. It would not be long now before the French fleet would have enough steam pressure to get under way and try to fight its way out of the harbor.

For a nearly unbearable hour, none of the French captains reappeared on the deck of the *Duquesne*. They were still belowdecks when Cunningham received a signal from Godfroy requesting permission to come aboard the *Warspite*. The French admiral, "with great dignity," announced that he was yielding to the "overwhelming force" of the Royal Navy. All of the ships in his fleet would, in the words of the formal agreement he thereupon signed, "be placed immediately in a condition in which they cannot fight."

The French fleet in Alexandria was neutralized, and saved to fight another day on the side of the Allies. "Never in my life," wrote Cunningham, "have I experienced such a wholehearted feeling of thankful relief." With more than a little satisfaction, he received a repentant message from the Admiralty: "We offer you our most sincere congratulations. The Prime Minister also wishes his congratulations to be sent to you." It was even more gratifying to Cunningham that he had been able to avoid hostilities against his old friend René Godfroy. During the night after their agreement had been signed, Alexandria was visited by Italian bombers, and they were quickly driven off with the help of antiaircraft fire from the French warships.

Godfroy—"an honorable if obstinate man," Cunningham called him—continued to follow the fortunes of the Royal Navy with interest through the following months. Confined to a form of exile in Alexandria, seldom leaving his disarmed warship, he nevertheless sent a personal message to Cunningham after every battle in which his friend was engaged: "No success of the British fleet passed without his letter of congratulations," Cunningham recalled, and "no loss without his letter of sympathy."

There were many repercussions to Britain's attack on the French Navy. Two days later, on July 5, French bombers retaliated with a raid on Gibraltar, but all of their bombs fell harmlessly into the bay. On July 8, a British torpedo plane damaged the *Richelieu* at Dakar; persistent British concern over that powerful battleship led to an abortive raid on the port by British and Free French forces in September. The heavy loss of French lives and ships at Mers-el-Kebir left a legacy of bitterness among the French in North Africa.

Still, the reactions to the attack were not nearly as critical as British officials had feared. In the United States, Secretary of State Cordell Hull rejected a protest from the Vichy government; he declared that American public opinion backed the British—a sentiment widely shared in neutral countries. The Germans made no reprisals against the French.

In the final reckoning, Prime Minister Churchill's gamble had paid off. However difficult and painful the decision and the operation, most of the French Navy had been denied to the Axis in one stroke. Count Galeazzo Ciano, Italy's Foreign Minister, made an observation that would soon be confirmed in sorrow by the Italian Navy: "The fighting spirit of His British Majesty's Fleet is quite alive."

A TRAGIC ENCOUNTER BETWEEN ALLIES

Few episodes in the entire War were more poignant than the confrontation between former allies that began on the morning of July 3, 1940, when a force of British ships appeared off Mers-el-Kebir in Algeria, where a French fleet was harbored. France had surrendered eight days earlier, but the powerful French Navy was still on the loose, dispersed from Egypt to Martinique. Prime Minister Churchill had issued orders to neutralize the French warships—by force if necessary—to prevent them from falling into German hands. The French were equally determined to let no foreign nation, Axis or Allied, possess their ships.

At Mers-el-Kebir, the burden of resolving this dilemma fell on two opposing admirals, Sir James Somerville of the Royal Navy and Marcel Bruno Gensoul of France. Neither desired bloodshed, but each man had his orders.

The sight of the British warships stunned Gensoul's sailors. Would the British really attack? "The English are crazy, crazy, completely crazy!" one officer exclaimed. Lieut. Commander Jean Boutron, a gunnery officer, thought the possibility "as unimaginable as an earthquake, a volcanic eruption or the announcement of the end of the world."

Somerville sent an officer to Gensoul with an ultimatum offering five choices: join your ships to the British fleet, sail to a British port and hand them over, sail them under guard to a neutral port, or scuttle them at once; otherwise we will sink them. Gensoul found it "absolutely impossible for me to bend to an ultimatum under the threat of English guns." Resolving to meet force with force, he ordered his ships to get up steam and prepare for action.

On board the Bretagne, Commander Boutron watched as the crewmen shuffled to their battle stations. "No orders were barked as is usual during maneuvers," he later wrote. "The men who saluted me wore glum, lifeless expressions. I told myself that it resembled a ballet on a phantom ship more closely than preparing to get under way."

The French ships took six hours to get up steam. All the while, the British emissary was frantically trying to win an audience with Admiral Gensoul and avoid a tragic battle.

The principals at Mers-el-Kebir were Admiral Somerville (left), ordered to neutralize the French ships, and Admiral Gensoul, who refused to give in.

AN ULTIMATUM DELIVERED TO A FRIEND

The British envoy to Admiral Gensoul was French-speaking Captain Cedric Holland, and he spent most of July 3 bobbing about in a launch in the harbor, waiting for a chance to present Britain's case personally to Gensoul. For more than seven hours, Gensoul refused to see him; the admiral sent aides to complain that the whole pro-

cedure was "an insult and a disgrace." Holland persevered. Finally, in the afternoon, Gensoul agreed to allow Holland to board the *Dunkerque* (right). The two men went straight to the point. Gensoul tried to assure the British that they had nothing to fear from the French ships: "I have orders to sink my ships to prevent their falling into German or Italian hands."

"The British government," Holland replied, "is unable to accept those orders as a sufficient guarantee."

"Do you not trust my word of honor?" Gensoul demanded.

"Of course we trust you," Holland answered, but "we do not trust the Germans or the Italians."

Gensoul was unmoved by Holland's arguments. The French battleships were still moored in a row (above) when Somerville at last ordered his fleet to open fire. Thus the British, as a French officer predicted, had "a firing exercise. A school for gunnery. Quite simply, an assassination."

Four French warships lie moored at the jetty, their sterns toward the sea and vulnerable to attack. The ships are (from left) the Dunkerque, the Provence, the Strasbourg and the Bretagne. An old seaplane tender, the Commandante Teste, lies at far right.

British Captain Holland and his aide leave the French flagship Dunkerque at 5.25 p.m. after a last, desperate attempt to persuade Admiral Gensoul to neutralize his ships. Half an hour later, the British began firing.

AGONIZING LAST MOMENTS ABOARD DOOMED SHIPS

... from the British fleet dropped another to the 26,500-ton Dunkerque. The first shell hit the work party ... whatever was trying to free the French battle cruiser's lines, and a second hit a tugboat that was struggling to pull the ship from her moorings, breaking the towline. Another shell demolished the Dunkerque's steering gear and quickly transformed her into an inferno of flame, smoke and screaming steam.

Three more shells plunged through the ... exploding in the ... flooded below ... in the engine rooms, the men were killed by live steam or drowning when the compartment flooded. The ship's electricity was knocked out, and ... were left smothering cold ... of a wrecked pier. ... through the harbor and beached herself.

The battleship Bretagne fared worse—much worse. At the first hit, recalled gunnery officer Boutron, the 28-year-old ship trembled from "a blow that I felt throughout my body." The second hit "was much stronger and the trembling became more violent." Then the Bretagne was shattered by tremendous explosions—the after ammunition magazine had blown up. "The enormous vessel was thrown into the air," remembered sailor Rudy Cantel.

The Bretagne began to sink, and those who could abandoned ship. "The men no longer had to jump into the water," Boutron said, "but only slide along the nearly vertical hull." The ship turned turtle and, with a massive shiver, slid beneath the water, taking three quarters of her crew with her. Sailors tried to rescue survivors from the water, but some of them were so badly wounded, said seaman Cantel, they "preferred to die."

ESCAPE FROM A HARBOR OF DEATH

Barely 15 minutes after it began, the British bombardment ended, with a total of only thirty-six 15-inch shells spent. The French tried bravely to return the fire, but were quickly knocked out of action.

The battle was over. The ordeal, however, was not over. Crewmen from the Bretagne who had managed to abandon ship struggled to stay afloat and reach more seaworthy boats with which to flee. Many, gasping for air, swallowed globs of oil and died after reaching them. One led Bouton gulped in oil and survived only because his rescuer, a fellow crewman, forced him to vomit.

Other victims were pulled from the sea by crewmen from the Commandant Teste, which had miraculously escaped being hit. Others were saved by a brave pilot from the Dunkerque who dived to pull exhausted men to the surface. But many drowning, oil-coated arms slipped from their would-be rescuers.

A third French warship was also hit, but the fourth managed to leave. Her boilers nearly exploded in heroic resolve. British eyes by the daring of those that now blockaded Strasbourg, steamed out of the harbor, enraged by a torpedo from the British destroyer, out to open sea and had to flee.

Admiral Somerville learned that the Strasbourg had planes from the carrier to pursue. Two flights of six with the French ship but her and the Strasbourg the port of Toulon in most

A British aerial torpedo smashes into the beached battle cruiser Dunkerque, sending up an oily geyser.

A FINISHING BLOW AND A MASS FAREWELL

Even as survivors of the shattered French fleet buried their 1,297 dead comrades, a second act of the tragedy of Mers-el-Kebir began. The day after the attack the commander in chief of the French Atlantic fleet, Admiral Jean-Pierre Estéva, with the hope of assuaging the pride of the French Navy, issued a public announcement stating that "the damage to the Dunkerque is minimal and the ship will soon be repaired." Estéva's statement served merely to bring the British back to finish the job. On the 6th of July, three waves of Royal Navy planes blasted the unfortunate battle cruiser and other targets in the harbor.

Despite the one-sided carnage, Admiral Gensoul believed that he had acted correctly. "It is my conviction," he later said, "that no French admiral would have accepted the terms of this ultimatum, not an English admiral, not an American admiral, no man in charge of a fleet."

Most of the French sailors damned the British for the attack. One seaman was so bitter that he took a straight razor and sliced a tattooed Union Jack off his arm. But some Navy men understood the British dilemma and forgave the attack. As Jean Boutron saw it, "The enemy were the Germans and not the English," and either "the English win the War and we win it with them, or we all are lost."

BRITAIN'S INVALUABLE ROCK

A Royal Navy flying boat wings past the towering Rock of Gibraltar, guardian of the western gateway to the Mediterranean at the southern tip of Spain.

The intricate, 10-mile-long labyrinth of tunnels and chambers that honeycomb Gibraltar is revealed on this map, based on information that was classified until 1978. The red lines show the maze of underground hospitals, ammunition magazines and waterworks that made the Rock such a formidable fortress. Above-ground features are shaded gray.

A GATEWAY GUARDED BY A LIMESTONE LABYRINTH

The embattled Allies owed an incalculable debt to Britain's fortress, Gibraltar, the rocky promontory that trails from the southern coast of Spain. Ceded to Britain as the spoils of war in 1713, Gibraltar is only three miles long and three quarters of a mile wide, yet it proved to be a key outpost in the Mediterranean theater. A solid limestone knob some 1,400 feet high, the Rock gave the British control of the vital 14-mile-wide strait that links the Atlantic and the Mediterranean. Gibraltar's ships, planes and guns protected convoys bound for Malta and the Middle East, kept the German surface navy out of the Mediterranean, bottled Italian warships inside, and blocked the Axis partners from using Spain as a shortcut to northwest Africa.

The Germans were keenly aware of Gibraltar's strategic value. Soon after the Wehrmacht crushed France in June 1940, Hitler approved an assault on the Rock via Spain, and crack German troops began rehearsing for the attack. However, the British had anticipated such a move. Since 1939 they had been working nonstop to redouble the Rock's defenses, creating a subterranean fortress with hundreds of guns, tanks to hold 16 million gallons of fresh water and enough supplies to withstand a year's siege.

The attack never came because Spain refused passage to Axis troops. Gibraltar's guns continued to command the strait and protect the harbor and the airfield built on the flat isthmus connecting the Rock to Spain. That airstrip assumed enormous importance as the War progressed. In 1942, as Allied plans matured for Operation *Torch,* the invasion of North Africa, the British high command realized that Gibraltar was the only spot in the western Mediterranean from which land-based planes could give cover for the Morocco- and Tunisia-bound assault fleet. Eight months of crash-paced building extended the airstrip's runway by 1,260 feet to accommodate the Allies' biggest bombers.

When *Torch* began, the Rock was ready. "Britain's Gibraltar," General Eisenhower later wrote, "made possible the invasion of northwest Africa." That invasion was the beginning of the end of Axis power in the Mediterranean.

A Royal Engineer floats on a raft (left) and another stands on a limestone outcropping as they inspect a 70,000-gallon lake found deep inside Gibraltar.

A pair of expert miners prepare gelignite charges that will be tamped into holes drilled by their fellow tunnelers and then detonated. Even while underground, the miners kept rifles handy in case of enemy invasion.

DIGGING IN AGAINST AN EXPECTED SIEGE

Gibraltar's defensive system of tunnels and gunports was begun by British military engineers during the Great Siege that started in 1779, when the Rock's British defenders held off some 40,000 French and Spanish attackers for almost four years.

Facing another possible siege in World War II, the British began in 1940 to extend the two-mile system another eight miles. This monumental task fell to four companies of the Royal Engineers—men who were miners in civilian life. These veterans, working in eight-hour shifts around the clock, indefatigably drilled holes in the Rock's limestone with hand-held drills, then filled the holes with the potent explosive gelignite. The resulting debris was used to build Gibraltar's airfield. Drilling and blasting were tedious; even the best crews could advance a tunnel an average of only 10 feet per shift. The work was still going on, in fact, at the end of the War.

A steam shovel and two dump trucks clear an immense spoil heap left

behind by tunnelers who blasted out this cavernous chamber within Gibraltar. The largest subterranean chambers were about 380 feet long and 50 feet wide.

A Black Watch trooper sights his Bren gun through a small gunport hidden on the northern side of Gibraltar. The battalion mascot also stands guard.

A heavy 9.2-inch gun points toward Spain from Breakneck Battery, high on Gibraltar's central ridge above the harbor.

THE LONG WATCH OF THE BLACK WATCH

The muscle of Gibraltar's 12,500-man defense included the 4th Battalion of the famous Black Watch Regiment. These tough Scottish soldiers had fought in France in 1940, had escaped from Dunkirk and, after only a few weeks in England, had been dispatched to isolated Gibraltar.

On arriving they found a mostly hostile environment: The jagged ridges and dizzyingly steep flanks of the Rock inflicted a severe case of vertigo on more than one soldier. The troops slept in caves and tun-nels, their nights interrupted repeatedly by the explosions of the tunnelers' charges.

Most oppressive to these professional soldiers was the lack of action, especially after Hitler's invasion of the Soviet Union in June 1941 drew away the Wehrmacht troops that might have assaulted the Rock. But the Black Watch nevertheless kept a keen lookout for much of the War, and some soldiers who had mining experience joined the tunneling crews to keep busy. In 1944 many of the Black Watch members were finally transferred to other units and got what they had been pining for—frontline combat duty during the invasion of Occupied France.

Escaping Gibraltar's broiling summer heat, British soldiers cool off in a pool constructed on the Rock's saw-toothed upper ridge.

Royal Navy visitors in tropical dress spend their liberty hours sauntering up and down the main street of Gibraltar's small town.

Royal Navy visitors in tropical dress spend their liberty hours sauntering up and down the main street of Gibraltar's small town.

Off-duty troops sprawl on cots in one of the cavernous barracks that were carved out of Gibraltar's cold and damp limestone rock.

A DAY-TO-DAY BATTLE AGAINST BOREDOM

Off-duty time on Gibraltar was only slightly less boring than the uneventful hours spent manning the Rock's defenses. For relief from torrid summer temperatures the troops could bathe at a few pools and small, sandy beaches—though not at the one set aside for the WRENS, members of the Women's Royal Naval Service. The men spent most of their free time in the cool underground barracks, reading, writing letters and playing cards.

The best hope for diversion, Gibraltar's tiny town, was quaint but disappointing. Most of its 20,000 civilians had been evacuated to the English countryside or the Azores during the perilous days of 1940. The men had little to do but window-shop or watch one another stroll aimlessly past.

At Gibraltar's main gate, a British border guard and his Spanish counterparts watch as a Bren-gun carrier rumbles out on patrol.

CLOSING THE GATE ON AXIS AGENTS

Security was a constant concern on Gibraltar. The rocky fortress was separated from the Spanish mainland by a minefield and a fence, and each day some 10,000 Spanish citizens from the nearby town of La Línea poured through a single gate to work in Gibraltar's construction gangs and to operate its shops. The British feared that German agents, numerous in Spain, might recruit workers as spies or saboteurs.

A few Axis agents did get past the rigorous border checks and patrols. One, Luis López Cordón-Cuenca, hid a powerful explosive device in the fruit shop where he worked, intending to detonate it inside a magazine full of ammunition for the upcoming Allied landings in Sicily. Acting on a tip, British security police foiled López' plan. He became one of three Axis spies on Gibraltar to be arrested, convicted and executed under wartime sedition laws.

In a rare photograph of an arrest, in 1943, Inspector William Adamson of the Gibraltar Security Police has collared Axis spy and would-be saboteur Luis López Cordón-Cuenca.

A view from the Spanish side of the border fence reveals a British pillbox with portholes and, behind it, the Rock's northern face.

Crewmen of the Royal Australian Air Force mark time beside a Wellington bomber while another of the twin-engined aircraft takes off from Gibraltar's airfield

on a patrol mission. The Wellingtons, slow but extremely reliable, flew far out over the Mediterranean and the Atlantic on forays against Axis submarines.

2

For Britain's Admiral Cunningham, the neutralization of the French Navy was an empty triumph. His fleet, deprived of the French warships, was now seriously outnumbered and stretched dangerously thin throughout the Mediterranean. According to his information, the Italians had one more battleship than he did, 15 more cruisers, 35 more fleet destroyers and about 100 more submarines. The admiral did have an aircraft carrier, whereas Italy had none.

The lack of aircraft carriers caused no little concern among the Supermarina—the high command of Italy's Navy. The admirals had been assured by Mussolini and by his all-services supreme command that the Regia Aeronautica—the Italian Air Force—would provide the Navy with long-range reconnaissance and air cover in case of a sea battle, and they hoped it was true. But they remained reluctant to commit their fleet to battle for another, more compelling reason.

The Italian warships in service in July of 1940 had been built or remodeled chiefly for speed and striking power. Most were three to five knots faster than their British counterparts, and their guns generally had longer ranges. But the trade-off for these assets had been a critical sacrifice in defensive strength. With the exception of the most modern class, the Italian cruisers were protected by armor so thin that many officers called them "the cardboard fleet."

Admiral Inigo Campioni, Commander in Chief of the Navy, and his Supermarina staff were capable, conservative officers, and the strategy they had evolved took full account of their fleet's shortcomings. They would rely heavily on their many submarines and torpedo boats, and conserve their major warships to escort convoys of supplies and troop reinforcements to the Italian armies fighting in North Africa. Between these swift escort forays, the greater part of the fleet would stay safe and sound behind the defensive installations of its main base, Taranto, inside the heel of the Italian boot.

It was clear to the Supermarina that Malta, in the narrow waters between Sicily and Libya, was the key to the control of the Mediterranean. As long as the island remained in British hands, it would be a bone in Italy's throat: The British planes and warships based there could ravage Italian convoys southbound for Libya and shield their own convoys eastbound for Alexandria. On the other hand, if Malta were

LIGHTNING STRIKE AT TARANTO

neutralized—or better yet captured—Italian sea and air units would inflict such devastating losses on the British convoys that the Mediterranean would be virtually closed to Allied shipping. Thus on June 11, 1940, just a day after Mussolini declared war, Italian bombers from airfields in Sicily began shuttling the 70 miles to Malta, pounding RAF bases and the Grand Harbor at Valletta.

Like the Italians, Cunningham realized the crucial importance of Malta—that the struggle for the Mediterranean would boil down to a battle of convoys and would be decided by possession of the island. He had made Malta his main base in 1939 even though the commanders of the British Army and the Royal Air Force had argued that the island was too exposed to be defended and that it would have to be abandoned. Cunningham insisted that Malta must be held, and the Admiralty in London permitted him to try.

The prospects of keeping the island seemed bleak in the first month of Mediterranean hostilities. The Italian air raids—72 in 29 days—made Malta so hazardous that the British Admiralty quickly ordered the surface warships there to move to Alexandria. Then, on July 7, 1940, freed for action by the immobilization of the French squadron in Alexandria 72 hours earlier, Cunningham and his fleet steamed out of the harbor and set course northwest for Malta to evacuate his headquarters personnel and his family. The aggressive admiral hoped to bump into the Italian fleet along the way and bring it to battle.

Soon after his fleet departed Alexandria, Cunningham received exciting news. The British submarine *Phoenix* radioed that she had sighted a sizable Italian Naval force 200 miles east of Malta heading south toward Africa, possibly to protect a convoy that was skirting the coastline en route to Libya. Cunningham asked Malta to send out a plane to shadow the Italians. Then he turned his force in order to get between the Italians and their home base at Taranto.

Cunningham's fleet also had been observed, and soon it was struck by Regia Aeronautica bombers flying from the Italian-owned Dodecanese Islands off the coast of Turkey. The Italian airmen preferred high-altitude bombing attacks, staying at 12,000 feet to reduce the effectiveness of British antiaircraft fire. Yet even from that height their marksmanship was remarkably accurate. During the British fleet's first full day at sea, July 8, an Italian bomb scored a direct hit on the compass platform of the cruiser *Gloucester*, killing her captain and 17 crewmen and crippling her steering gear.

By midafternoon the observation plane sent from Malta had reported that the Italian fleet consisted of two battleships, six cruisers and seven destroyers, and that it had turned north. Apparently the warships had escorted the convoy to Libya and were now heading back to port. Hoping to cut them off, Cunningham headed for the instep of the Italian boot.

After a tense night, Cunningham dispatched three planes from his carrier *Eagle* to locate the enemy. These planes and others from Malta reported that the Italians were still running for Taranto and that they had been joined by supporting forces: six more cruisers and 13 more destroyers. The British closed in rapidly. When sighted by the planes just after dawn, the enemy fleet was 145 miles to the west. By noon Cunningham had shortened the distance to 90 miles.

"It was not quite the moment I would have chosen to give battle," Cunningham later admitted, for the Italians outnumbered his force and most of his ships had used up half their antiaircraft ammunition fighting off the attacks of the day before. But to the pugnacious Cunningham "any opportunity was welcome." He sent off a wave of torpedo bombers, followed by his fast cruisers, and took his flagship *Warspite* in to support the cruisers.

The Action off Calabria, as the engagement was later known, proved to be a textbook battle for the British. The enemy fleet, sighted by a submarine, was tracked by land-based aircraft and its position was pinpointed by carrier-based reconnaissance planes. The torpedo bombers were dispatched and the forward line of cruisers steamed in for the first shots. Finally the battleships advanced, bringing up the biggest guns.

It was a perfect day for the affray, with visibility of 20 miles. The British lookouts searched the horizon for signs of the first enemy ship. At 3:08 on the afternoon of July 9, the cruiser *Neptune* signaled the message, "Enemy battle fleet in sight." It was the first time this warning had been sent by a British vessel in the Mediterranean since the warship *Zealous* had flagged the alert to Lord Nelson 142 years earlier at the Battle of the Nile.

Six minutes after the *Neptune's* signal, four Italian cruisers opened fire. Their 8-inch guns had a longer range than those of the British cruisers bearing down on them, but the British fire was so accurate it rattled the Italian gunners and spoiled their aim. Then the *Warspite* steamed into action, shuddering under the recoil of her big 15-inch guns.

Cunningham could now see the Italian warships coming over the horizon, firing as they approached. The range was great—26,000 yards, or about 15 miles—but the exploding shells straddled the *Warspite*. Cunningham's flagship returned fire, and the battleship *Malaya* soon arrived to add her guns to the British broadsides.

When a shell from one of the *Warspite's* 15-inchers land-ed at the base of the foremost funnel of the distant Italian flagship *Giulio Cesare*, Cunningham, watching through his binoculars, saw "the great orange-colored flash of a heavy explosion" followed by a rising pall of black smoke.

This hit at long range was too much for Admiral Campioni, who took his wounded flagship behind a heavy smoke screen. One by one the other Italian warships followed, and by 5 p.m. the enemy fleet had vanished.

Cunningham was frustrated by the Italians' retreat; it was too dangerous to pursue them into the narrow, mined Strait of Messina between Sicily and the Italian mainland, so the British turned back. The *Warspite's* long-range hit had failed

Five Savoia-Marchetti bombers fly in close formation as they search for the Royal Navy's Mediterranean fleet. The trimotored aircraft, which also served as transports, were the work horses of the Italian Air Force.

to sink the *Giulio Cesare*, but it was to have "a moral effect quite out of proportion to the damage," Cunningham later observed: Never again would the Italian Navy willingly confront the fire of British battleships.

By the time the battle ended, the evacuation from Malta had commenced. Cunningham detached part of his fleet to reinforce the evacuation convoys and hurried on ahead for a conference in Cairo. The convoys got through to Alexandria with only minor damage from Italian air attacks. Lady Cunningham, arriving safely in Alexandria harbor, was relieved to see the *Warspite* already moored there, and to find the admiral suffering only from disappointment at the Italians' escape.

Despite his modest success off Calabria, Cunningham was worried about the size and condition of his forces. Two of his battleships were old and his one aircraft carrier, the *Eagle*, was an antique; built as a battleship before World War I, she had been given an improvised flight deck in 1923. Cunningham began bombarding the Admiralty with requests for more ships and more planes.

The Sea Lords in London at last decided to send two antiaircraft cruisers, the 26-year-old but modernized battleship *Valiant* and, best of all, the fast new carrier *Illustrious*. Unlike the *Eagle*, the *Illustrious* had the protection of an armor-plated flight deck *(pages 65-67)*. Further, she was equipped with that marvelous new device, radar, and a Canadian expert who could make sense of the mystifying little blips on the radar screen.

These reinforcements reached Gibraltar on August 29, escorted by warships under Vice Admiral Sir James Somerville, in command of Force H in the western Mediterranean. Under cover of darkness, the force sailed safely through the perilous strait between Malta and Sicily. Cunningham's squadron met Somerville and his charges just south of Malta and escorted them to Alexandria.

Cunningham's augmented fleet still did not equal the Italian Navy in battleships and cruisers, but with two aircraft carriers on hand, the admiral felt certain he could defeat the enemy in an all-out naval battle. His problem was that the Italian fleet, following its cautious strategy, emerged from its Taranto base only sporadically to escort convoys to North Africa, and then steamed swiftly home.

Then Cunningham was deflected from his main objective of crippling the Italian fleet. On September 13, the Italian armies of Marshal Rodolfo Graziani thrust eastward through the Western Desert of Libya, driving the British forces of General Sir Archibald Wavell across the border into Egypt and toward Alexandria, 200 miles distant. In this crisis Cunningham dispatched his destroyers to bombard Graziani's supply lines along the coastal roads, as well as large Italian depots at Bardia and elsewhere. In the meantime, the admiral formed the nucleus of an Inshore Squadron, whose little gunboats—named the *Ladybird,* the *Aphis* and the *Gnat*—harassed enemy trucks and troop concentrations. Graziani halted his advance at Sidi Barrani because he did not want to further expose his supply lines to British attacks from the sea.

Despite these demands on his forces, Cunningham kept looking for the main Italian fleet. In late September, some 10 weeks after the encounter off the Calabrian coast, a British force on convoy duty spotted and pursued an Italian flotilla. The Italians, though much better armed, ducked into Taranto before they could be engaged. Then in early October, Cunningham's fleet escorted a convoy into the central Mediterranean with the express purpose of luring the Italians out. He managed a petty skirmish with a few destroyers, but the Italian battleships stayed safely in port, their commanders carefully following the orders of the Naval Chief of Staff, Admiral Domenico Cavagnari, to avoid confronting the British fleet.

Cavagnari realized that the British aircraft carriers gave Cunningham's fleet a flexibility the Italians sorely needed. Even in the cozy confines of the Mediterranean, shore-based aircraft could not always reach an enemy fleet, and Cavagnari had no intention of permitting his battleships to be caught at sea by torpedo planes from the *Eagle* or the newly arrived *Illustrious*. Disregarding the dismay and resentment of his aggressive younger officers, Cavagnari kept his big ships in the harbor of Taranto.

By mid-October, Cunningham had come to a momentous decision: If the Italian ships would not come out, he would go in after them—with aircraft. And as it happened, the man who had brought the *Illustrious* from England to Alexandria was Rear Admiral Lumley Lyster, a hawk-nosed sailor with a well-devised plan for just such a surprise blow.

The plan was not new. A naval air strike at Taranto had been worked out as a contingency plan for the carrier *Glorious* in 1935, during Mussolini's invasion of Ethiopia. Since England had not gone to war over that bit of aggression, the scheme had been put aside. But in 1938, when Lumley Lyster was captain of the *Glorious*, the plan had turned up in the ship's files, and he had not forgotten it. Upon his arrival in the Mediterranean, Lyster sketched out the strike for his new commander, and Admiral Cunningham quickly gave him the go-ahead.

The plan was daring in the extreme—suicidal, some called it at first. Carrier-based torpedo planes were supposed to reach the enemy fleet's main anchorage at Taranto undetected. They would skim low across the harbor, release their deadly projectiles just a few hundred yards from the anchored Italian capital ships, then zoom away through a hail of antiaircraft fire.

The dangers of the attack were increased by the limitations of the aircraft Lyster would have to use. The Swordfish *(pages 70-71),* manufactured by the Fairey Aviation Company, was a fabric-covered, open-cockpit biplane. It looked so flimsy that a visiting American airman, upon seeing the plane for the first time, exclaimed, ''My God, you don't mean to say you fly those things!'' With a maximum speed of only 139 miles per hour, the Swordfish made such an easy target that the attack plan called for a mission under cover of night—with all the hazards entailed in carrier operations in the dark.

Lyster, an informal officer who often dressed in an old turtleneck sweater and a battered yachting cap, immediately began putting the fleet's most experienced Swordfish crews through grueling nighttime drills. The pilots practiced plummeting down to wavetop level, then making short runs toward dummy targets. The observer-navigators learned to stuff themselves into rear cockpits along with the bulky 60-gallon auxiliary fuel tanks that would be needed for the long overwater flight; there was no room left for the plane's third crew member, the gunner. In supervising these training sessions Lyster was aided by the *Illustrious'* air officer, Ian Robertson, a fanatic for speed and efficiency who was known to all aboard as ''Streamline.''

Lyster planned to send at least two dozen Swordfish across the Gulf of Taranto in two waves an hour apart. The carrier would launch them some 170 miles from their objective. From the launch spot, Point X, each wave would fly to Taranto in formation, then split up; the Swordfish would dive toward their targets from different directions to distract the Italian antiaircraft gunners.

After weeks of furious preparation, Lyster and Robertson informed Cunningham that 30 aircrews and planes from the *Illustrious* and the *Eagle* were ready to go. Cunningham and Lyster studied the calendar and selected the night of October 21, when a full moon would help the pilots and navigators find Taranto—and help the survivors, if any, find their way back to the carriers. Since October 21 was Trafalgar Day, the anniversary of Nelson's crushing victory over Napoleon's navy, Cunningham considered it a fitting date for an attempt on Mussolini's fleet.

But this felicitous timetable soon fell victim to a freak mishap. A crewman fitting a supplementary fuel tank into a Swordfish's rear cockpit in the *Illustrious'* cavernous belowdecks hangar slipped on a grease spot and struck a pair of exposed electrical terminals with his metal screwdriver. A small spark detonated the gasoline fumes escaping from the tank. Flames quickly engulfed the Swordfish and another one nearby. Moments later, overhead extinguishers were spraying the planes and the hangar. A catastrophe was averted, but two of the precious Swordfish had been destroyed. All of the others were saturated with salt-water spray; they had to be taken apart, washed down with fresh water, dried, oiled and reassembled.

Working around the clock, the mechanics got the job done, but by then it was too late to stage the attack on Trafalgar Day. A new date, the 11th of November, was selected for its promise of a three-quarter moon. Cunningham assigned the attack a portentous code name: Operation *Judgement.* ''We all hoped,'' one of the pilots later wrote, ''that it was the Italians who were about to meet their Maker and not us.''

Meanwhile, the Royal Air Force was providing vital aerial photographs of Taranto. The pictures were taken by Squadron Leader Ernest Whiteley's 431st General Reconnaissance Flight, whose pilots made the 700-mile trip from Malta to Taranto and back every day. The 431st possessed a new, speedy American bomber, the Martin A-30 Baltimore,

THE ARMORED INNARDS OF THE "ILLUSTRIOUS"

The brain and the heart of the fleet aircraft carrier were its operations island above deck and its hangar system below. A prime example was the Royal Navy's *Illustrious*, commissioned in 1940 and the last word in carriers. Her hangar deck was a self-contained armored unit sealed within the armored hull of the ship. Three inches of steel flight deck formed the hangar's roof, a 4.5-inch steel bulkhead surrounded it, and three inches of steel deck protected against explosions in the boiler rooms below. Shutters on the fore and aft elevators that raised aircraft to the flight deck were similarly armored.

This great steel vault was mounted in the midship section of the hull, which was sheathed with another 4.5 inches of armor that reached five feet below the waterline. Beneath it ran a series of watertight com-

partments built to absorb the shock of torpedoes. Even the aviation gas was stored in steel cylinders immersed in water tanks.

This extensive protection saved the *Illustrious* from sinking in January 1941, when the Luftwaffe, in repeated attacks on the carrier, scored eight direct hits and seven near misses. The *Illustrious* and her planes survived to fight again.

In this cross section of the Illustrious, the armored hangar deck and its aircraft, wings folded, lie just beneath the flight deck. On the right is the island and below are the boilers that drove the ship at a top speed of 31 knots.

1 *Armor*
2 *Safety-barrier mechanism*
3 *Swordfish with folded wings*
4 *Removable grating*
5 *Boiler-room vent and uptake*
6 *Passage*
7 *Life raft*
8 *Net and antenna support*
9 *Washroom*
10 *Turbogenerator*
11 *Fuel-oil tank*
12 *Water-tank*
13 *Bilge keel*
14 *Docking keel*
15 *Ballast space*
16 *Boiler*
17 *Firebrick storage*
18 *Electrical-cable passage*
19 *First-aid equipment*

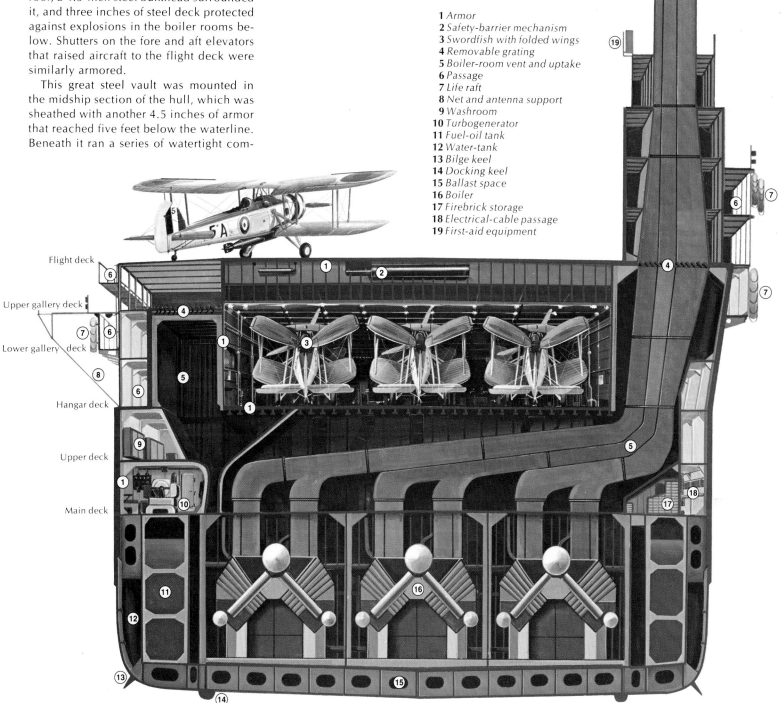

Flight deck
Upper gallery deck
Lower gallery deck
Hangar deck
Upper deck
Main deck

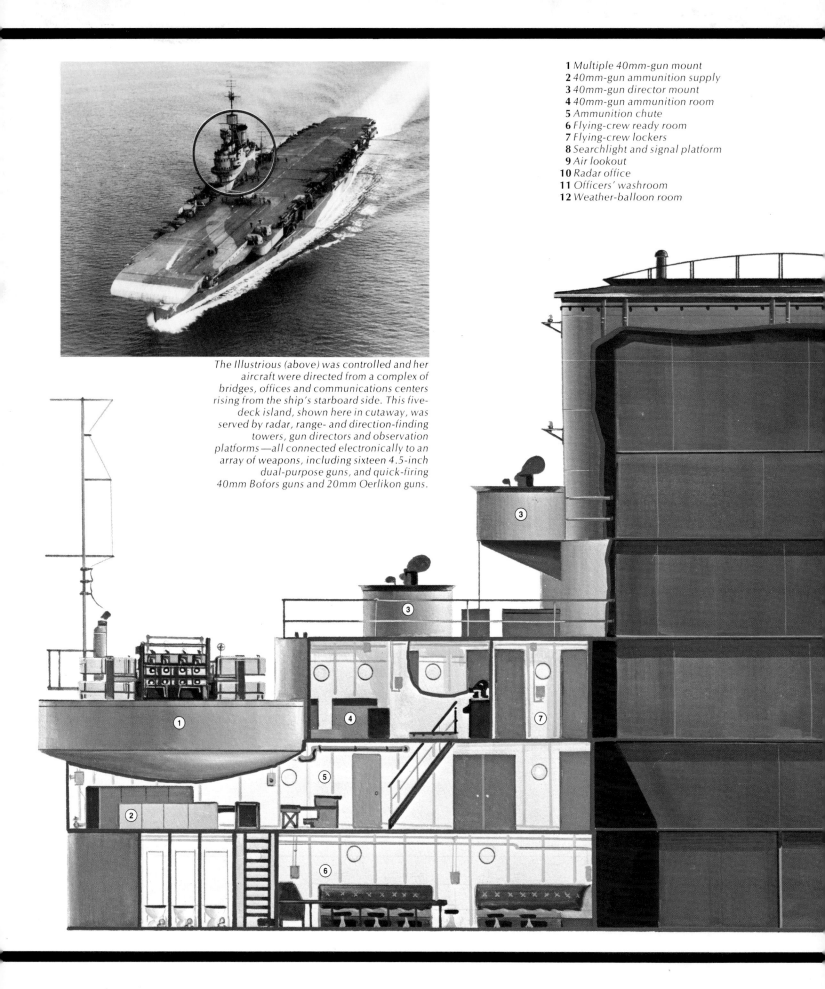

1 Multiple 40mm-gun mount
2 40mm-gun ammunition supply
3 40mm-gun director mount
4 40mm-gun ammunition room
5 Ammunition chute
6 Flying-crew ready room
7 Flying-crew lockers
8 Searchlight and signal platform
9 Air lookout
10 Radar office
11 Officers' washroom
12 Weather-balloon room

The Illustrious (above) was controlled and her aircraft were directed from a complex of bridges, offices and communications centers rising from the ship's starboard side. This five-deck island, shown here in cutaway, was served by radar, range- and direction-finding towers, gun directors and observation platforms—all connected electronically to an array of weapons, including sixteen 4.5-inch dual-purpose guns, and quick-firing 40mm Bofors guns and 20mm Oerlikon guns.

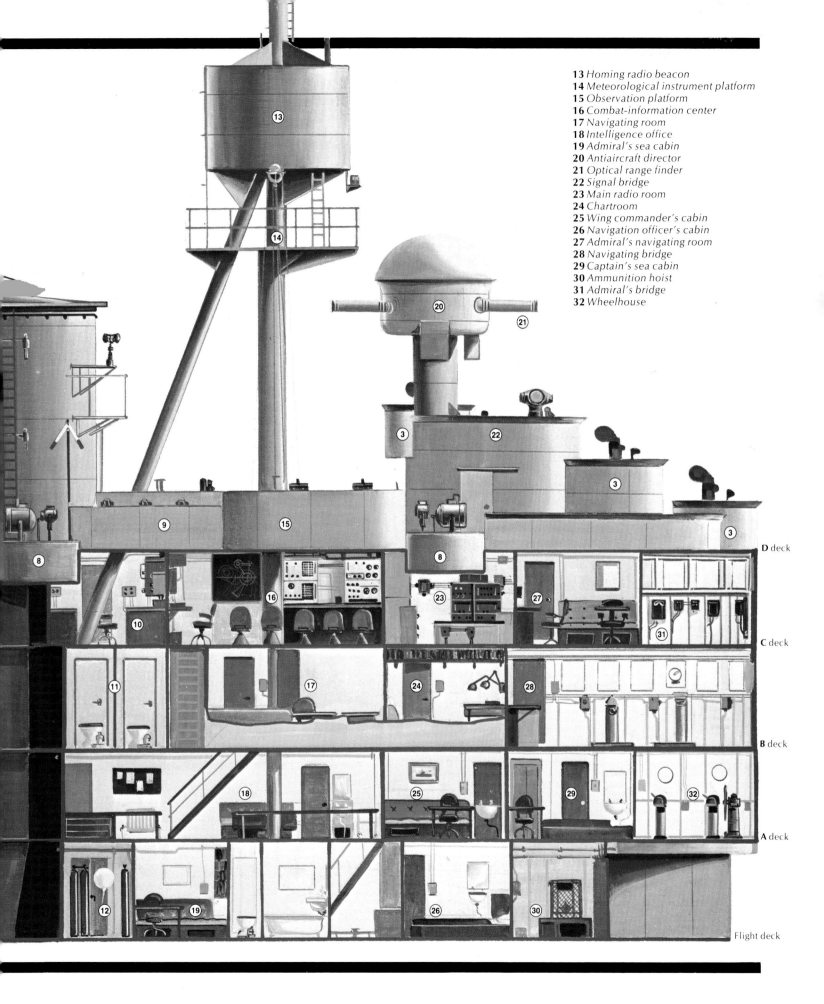

13 *Homing radio beacon*
14 *Meteorological instrument platform*
15 *Observation platform*
16 *Combat-information center*
17 *Navigating room*
18 *Intelligence office*
19 *Admiral's sea cabin*
20 *Antiaircraft director*
21 *Optical range finder*
22 *Signal bridge*
23 *Main radio room*
24 *Chartroom*
25 *Wing commander's cabin*
26 *Navigation officer's cabin*
27 *Admiral's navigating room*
28 *Navigating bridge*
29 *Captain's sea cabin*
30 *Ammunition hoist*
31 *Admiral's bridge*
32 *Wheelhouse*

D deck

C deck

B deck

A deck

Flight deck

which was manufactured in Baltimore, Maryland. A number of these twin-engined aircraft had been crated and sent to France early in 1940. To escape the German blitzkrieg that knocked France out of the War, the crates were diverted to England, where the RAF assembled the planes, renamed them Marylands, and sent three of them winging off to Malta as reconnaissance craft to scout the Mediterranean. They proved superior to Britain's lumbering Sunderland flying boats; the Marylands roared over their targets at 270 miles per hour and snapped their pictures before the Italian antiaircraft gunners could get their range.

The photographs of Taranto taken by the Marylands were dispatched to Cairo, where the Royal Air Force maintained its Middle Eastern photo-interpretation headquarters. There, Navy Lieutenant David Pollock, Admiral Lyster's young intelligence and operations officer, decided to study the aerial

Captain Denis Boyd of the carrier Illustrious combined his abilities as a pilot, an aerial photographer and a torpedo expert in directing the torpedo-bomber attack that savaged the Italian fleet at Taranto harbor.

photographs through an old-fashioned stereopticon, hoping to learn more about the target by examining it in depth. Two photos of the same area taken from slightly different angles, when placed side by side in the twin-lensed viewer, suddenly leaped into three-dimensional relief. Pollock pored over a set of views of Taranto that had been taken from 16,000 feet. There were the tempting rows of Italian destroyers and cruisers and, as expected, five big battleships, all anchored in Taranto's outer harbor, known as the Mar Grande (Great Sea).

But there was also something about the pictures that bothered Pollock: small white flecks that at first looked as though they might be blemishes on the prints, or perhaps spots on the camera's lenses. They seemed too regularly spaced, however, to be random imperfections. And the stereopticon made them seem to rise off the print. Then it dawned on Pollock: They must be barrage balloons, small gas-filled blimps floating at the end of steel cables that would slice the wing off a low-flying plane.

These neat rows of balloons were a new element that clearly called for a change of plan. Pollock asked the RAF duty officer to lend him the prints long enough to fly them from Cairo to Alexandria. There he would show them to Captain Denis Boyd and other veteran airmen on board the Illustrious. But at this point Pollock ran into a tangle of red tape. The duty officer forwarded Pollock's request to the group captain, who bucked it all the way up the chain of command to Air Chief Marshal Sir Arthur Longmore, who said no; never did RAF reconnaissance photographs leave headquarters.

But Lieutenant Pollock was not to be stopped. He simply waited until the duty officer was preoccupied and then took the prints.

Pollock flew to Alexandria and showed the pictures to Captain Boyd, who agreed that the spots looked like barrage balloons; better show the photos to Cunningham himself. Rushing over to the Warspite, Pollock was intercepted by the flagship's staff officer, who looked at the photographs and told the lieutenant to show them to Cunningham's chief of staff, Rear Admiral Algernon Willis.

Reaching Willis' cabin, Pollock was greeted brusquely by the admiral, who had just emerged dripping wet from his shower. "And what the hell do you want?" Willis snapped.

Pollock insisted on showing him the prints. Willis thought the specks might be barrage balloons, but he was not convinced. Take the photos back to Cairo, he ordered, and get the RAF to forward an official interpretation of them to Admiral Cunningham.

Pollock hurried back aboard the *Illustrious* and had the ship's photographer make copies of his purloined prints so that Navy fliers would at least be able to study their targets. He then flew back to Cairo, slipped the pictures back into their drawer before they were missed, and obediently asked for official RAF interpretation. Shortly afterward the RAF report went through proper channels to Cunningham: The spots were indeed barrage balloons.

So the Swordfish pilots went back to the wardroom blackboard. The attack planners calculated that the balloons were some 300 yards apart. Although a Swordfish could fly between the obstructions, it would be extremely risky to attempt it at night at 130 miles per hour. A few attack lanes were plotted through the one apparent gap in the network. But in order to confuse antiaircraft fire by approaching the targets from several directions, some of the Swordfish would be required to fly through the balloon barrier. The other attack lanes were redrawn accordingly. And because of the new menace the balloons and their steel cables presented, it was determined that moonlight alone would not provide enough visibility. Some of the Swordfish would therefore

Italian ground crewmen at Taranto harbor prepare to launch one of the 87 hydrogen-filled barrage balloons whose heavy steel anchoring cables constituted an important part of the Naval base's network of air defenses.

carry magnesium flares and bombs instead of torpedoes; they would drop a line of flares on the eastern shore of the harbor to silhouette the targets for the torpedo-carrying planes arriving from the southwest and northwest. Then the flare-droppers would bomb the harbor installations before beating a retreat.

The 30 Swordfish originally assigned to the attack were gradually cut back by unforeseen developments. First came problems with the carrier *Eagle,* which was to sail to Point X with the *Illustrious* and launch her Swordfish there. This aged vessel was strained in every joint after a year of churning through the Mediterranean with Cunningham's fleet. She had often been attacked by shore-based planes and although no bomb had struck her, the numerous near misses had so shaken her old hull that her fuel lines were severely damaged. Since only an overhaul would rectify the problem, the *Eagle* remained behind in Alexandria. Fortunately, the *Illustrious* was able to crowd five of the *Eagle's* Swordfish into her hangar, and these were transferred. But the loss of the *Eagle's* other six aircraft cut the attack force to 24.

More mishaps occurred after the *Illustrious* had sailed from Alexandria and, in company with the bulk of Cunningham's fleet, was entering the central Mediterranean to watch for signs of Italian interference. On the 9th of November one of the carrier's Swordfish left the flight deck, had engine trouble and fell into the sea. The next day another Swordfish engine mysteriously failed, and on the following day yet another. All of the crewmen were rescued, but the three Swordfish were lost. The source of the trouble was discovered after the fuel tanks of the remaining aircraft had been hurriedly drained: One of the carrier's big supply tanks contained gasoline that had somehow become fouled with sand, water and algae; all three of the lost planes had been fueled from this tank. The mystery was solved, but three more precious Swordfish were gone. The attack force was now down to 21.

The Swordfish were divided into two waves, 12 in the first and nine in the second. The first wave would enjoy whatever element of surprise there might be. Six planes in this initial flight would carry one torpedo each, the standard 18-inch Mark XII model, set to run at 27 knots at a depth of 33 feet. The torpedoes would be fitted with a revolu-

The Fairey Swordfish, 36 feet long with foldable wings spanning 45 feet, was driven by a 690- or 750-horsepower Pegasus engine at a top speed of 139 knots. Stripped down and fitted with an extra gas tank, the torpedo bomber could range 1,030 miles at 104 knots to search out and track enemy vessels.

STURDY DOWAGER WITH A LETHAL STING

"This amiable dowager of an airplane," said a pilot of the Fairey Swordfish, "revealed amazonian proclivities" in combat. Indeed, the Royal Navy's dowdy-looking but versatile torpedo bomber performed every job in the Fleet Air Arm except flying fighter cover.

With its light but sturdy frame of fabric-covered steel tubing, the Swordfish was able to range 546 miles carrying a single 1,610-pound torpedo or 1,500 pounds of bombs. Depending upon its mission, the aircraft wielded an assortment of other ordnance and gear: eight 60-pound rockets or a 1,500-pound mine; flares, incendiary bombs and depth charges; twin pontoons for landings at sea, a searchlight and a radar dome. The Swordfish's capacity to fly anywhere and carry anything earned it the nickname "Stringbag," after the British housewife's compact but almost infinitely expandable shopping bag of knotted string.

Besides devastating the Italian fleet at Taranto in 1940, torpedo-carrying Swordfish crippled the German battleship *Bismarck* in 1941 and sank an average of 50,000 tons of Mediterranean shipping per month during 1940 and 1941. Swordfish operating from Malta in 1942 sank 30 Axis ships in 36 night attacks. And the plane was even more useful against Axis submarines; its slow speed, long range and wealth of detection gear made it a lethal hunter-killer of U-boats right up to the end of the War.

tionary firing mechanism called the Duplex pistol—duplex because it would trigger the torpedoes either when they struck a ship's hull or when they passed into its magnetic field. This solved the problem posed by the heavy steel-mesh torpedo nets that were known to be spread around the Italian battleships. A torpedo could be set to run under the nets and still detonate when passing beneath the target. The pistol also contained a safety device to prevent the torpedo from exploding while it was attached to the plane or when it hit the water.

The battleships were the central targets. The latest aerial photographs had shown five of them clumped together as if in a shooting gallery. And as the *Illustrious* neared Point X on the afternoon of November 11, a plane winged in bearing the latest RAF reconnaissance photographs: They showed a sixth Italian battleship steaming into the harbor. "So all the pheasants," Admiral Cunningham later wrote, "had gone home to roost."

At 6 p.m. on November 11, the *Illustrious,* her Swordfish ready and her men briefed, swung northeast toward the launching site 40 miles west of the Greek island of Cephalonia. Alongside the carrier steamed a protective screen of four cruisers and four destroyers.

By 7:30 the aircrews had finished their dinners, were drinking more coffee than usual and were chain-smoking what might be their last cigarettes. The dozen Swordfish of Squadron 815, the first wave, were being brought up one by one from the belowdecks hangar to sit at the stern, their cloth-covered wings still folded back. The 24 men who would lead the attack emerged onto the ship's darkened flight deck.

The big British carrier was hissing through the calm Ionian Sea at 28 knots. A three-quarter moon astern made her wake sparkle. A throng of plane handlers and mechanics swarmed around the Swordfish, helping the pilots and the navigators ease themselves and their bulky flying suits into the open cockpits of the biplanes. When the *Illustrious* reached Point X, 170 miles southeast of Taranto, she slowly wheeled into the light wind; the heavily laden aircraft would need every knot of wind over the carrier's deck for lift on takeoff.

At 8:10 a warning klaxon sounded. The pilots and navi-

gators tightened their parachute and harness straps and checked their instruments for the last time. One after another, propellers were swung. Engines whined, spat and roared. Plane handlers lying on the deck held the planes' wheel chocks in place while the pilots revved the engines. In a flash the flight-deck lights came on. At 8:35 there was a flicker of green light from a sponson just below the bridge as "Streamline" Robertson signaled "Chocks away!" to the first plane in line. Swordfish L4A lumbered down the deck, gradually picking up speed. Almost too soon it dropped off the bow, dipped nearly out of sight and then roared off into the night.

The next plane had already moved up to takeoff position, and Robertson quickly flashed his green light again. He had improved his takeoff teamwork in the past few months after a visiting U.S. Navy lieutenant had chided him over the *Illustrious'* 30-second interval between planes. "I'm pretty sure on our flattops we do it in 10," the American had said. Thereupon Robertson had trimmed the planes' takeoff interval to 10 seconds.

In a few minutes 12 Swordfish were airborne, nine of them climbing together to 7,500 feet; the other three, unable to locate the formation in the clouds and darkness, headed for Taranto on their own. For two hours and 20 minutes the planes droned northwestward, the moon silvering the light cloud cover.

When most of the planes were still 50 miles from their target, the crews saw the sky dead ahead erupt in multicolored gunfire: At least one Swordfish had arrived at Taranto prematurely. In fact, the Italian gunners were firing furiously at Ian Swayne, one of the three pilots who had failed to find the main formation, and who had flown his Swordfish to the target area at sea level. Since he had spent no time climbing, Swayne had reached Taranto 15 minutes ahead of schedule. The roar of his approaching engine had been detected by Italian sound equipment, giving the Taranto garrison its first inkling of the British presence. The antiaircraft artillery, which included 21 batteries of 4-inch guns, began to fill the skies with exploding shells. Swayne sensibly flew to and fro a safe distance from the shore and waited for the other planes to arrive.

At 11:02 the first of the flare-droppers began his run in the teeth of the Italian antiaircraft fire. The magnesium flares,

An aerial photograph of Taranto harbor taken the day after the British torpedo-bomber attack reveals half a dozen of the Italian Navy's finest warships lying submerged or still burning. The whitish line running irregularly across the harbor marks the edge of a slick of leaking fuel.

floating down under their small parachutes, sent a blaze of unearthly golden light over the anchored ships; the entire harbor was illuminated.

The lead torpedo plane pitched downward to begin its run. The commander of Squadron 815, leading this first wave in Swordfish L4A, was Lieutenant Kenneth Williamson, with N. J. Scarlett as his navigator. Williamson's attack lane led in over the harbor from the west, between steel cables that moored the barrage balloons. By the time his Swordfish had completed its steep attack dive, plunging from 7,500 feet to 750, it was whistling along at 145 knots. The red and blue balls of tracer fire that had been streaking below Williamson's plane suddenly seemed to be floating off above him; he was diving too fast for the gunners to track his aircraft. As he leveled off before making his last dip to water level, a steel cable flashed past; he was now inside the balloon defense line.

Swerving erratically in order to present a difficult target, Lieutenant Williamson sped across the harbor surface, its dark waters mirroring the shellbursts above him. He could hear the cracking thunder of the guns above the roar of his engine as he peered ahead for his target. The first object he distinguished was a sea wall; he recognized it from the briefing as the breakwater that protected the big ships' berth. Then he saw a looming line of gray steel with unmistakable battleship superstructures.

The antiaircraft guns on the Italian ships had joined the shore batteries in firing at the attacking planes. Two destroyers just ahead of Williamson were shooting so furiously that he was almost blinded. He turned to port and spotted a battleship dead ahead, its guns spurting flame. He headed straight for the flashes. Through a kaleidoscope of light and angry fire he jinked his plane across the water. His target loomed directly between the bars of his torpedo sight; just when it seemed that he would crash into her, he pressed the torpedo-release grip.

The Swordfish leaped upward as its ponderous torpedo dropped from the plane. Williamson, sure that he had made a direct hit, pulled back on the stick and kicked his rudder pedal. The Swordfish climbed swiftly to the right—and directly into a stream of gunfire. The plane shuddered, lost headway and plunged into the harbor.

Williamson was knocked unconscious by the crash, but the water revived him. He had time to unsnap his harness, swim to the surface and gasp for air. He found navigator Scarlett splashing alongside the plane, which was sinking in a flurry of oily bubbles. With machine-gun bullets peppering the water around them, the two airmen swam to the nearest dock, where they were taken prisoner by some Italian sailors. (They were treated almost like guests by the Italians. But after Italy capitulated in 1943, they spent the rest of the War living like ordinary POWs in a German prisoner-of-war camp.)

Williamson's plane, astonishingly, was the only one in the first wave to be shot down. His torpedo knocked the battleship Conte di Cavour out of the War. Another Sword-

Japanese Rear Admiral Koki Abe (second from left) tours Italian Navy facilities in May of 1941. Details he gathered about the British raid on Taranto were included in planning Japan's attack on Pearl Harbor seven months later.

fish in the first strike flew so close to its target that its navigator could see the wake of the torpedo streaking straight for the battleship *Littorio*. The navigator in Ian Swayne's plane watched their torpedo slam into its target only seconds after Swayne had pulled up from his wavetop approach run. The pilots of all six torpedo-carrying Swordfish came within feet of crashing into a ship or of having their aircraft cut in two by a balloon cable. Pilot Michael Maund flew in so low that he spent a few frantic moments twisting and turning like a trapped bird to avoid the masts of the vessels around him.

High above, the Swordfish pilots who had lighted the scene with flares flew on to bomb fuel tanks and port facilities in Taranto's inner harbor (Mar Piccolo). To one of the pilots, the torpedo planes below were "flopping about on the water's surface like grey moths." Another pilot, Charles Lamb, concluded that the torpedo planes were leading a charmed life because they were going in so low; the Italian gunners were firing high for fear of hitting their own ships or the town of Taranto. "Had the fire been maintained at water level," Lamb later wrote, "all six would have been shot to pieces within seconds."

Squadron 819, the second wave, arrived on schedule about an hour after the first. Again the torpedo-carrying planes screamed down to wave height to aim for the battleships. Pilot Frederick Torrens-Spence actually touched the water, his wheels skimming the waves like skipping stones. Pilot Charles S. Lea, pulling up after dropping his torpedo, passed so close to a cruiser that the concussion of her guns seemed to lift his plane.

At the peak of the second attack, two Swordfish pilots found themselves on a collision course. One dived just in time to avoid the other—who was almost immediately shot down. It was the only Swordfish lost in the second wave; both pilot and navigator were killed. The rest of the airmen in Squadron 819, looking back at Taranto as they headed home for the *Illustrious*, witnessed an inferno of burning ships, billowing smoke, and a harbor that had become a sea of flaming oil.

All but the two downed Swordfish made the return flight safely. Italian planes had failed to discover the whereabouts of the *Illustrious*, and she was waiting for her Swordfish off Cephalonia. One by one the pilots dropped softly onto her flight deck, to the cheers of the sailors and the congratulations of Admiral Lyster.

A short time later, a ringing telephone awakened Admiral Emilio Mariano, the Prefect of Taranto, who had gone to bed in shock and despair after the air attack ended.

The admiral picked up the phone and heard a familiar voice say, "Is that you, Mariano?"

"Yes, Duce," he said.

"Tell me, Mariano, what is the news?"

"It's been a very hard night, Duce," Mariano informed him. Then he reported that there had been heavy losses. Later, Mussolini received a full account from Admiral Cavagnari and a critical evaluation from the Supermarina. But the Duce's son-in-law, Count Galeazzo Ciano, wrote in his diary, "Mussolini seems not to have understood the gravity of the episode."

Indeed, the toll was staggering. Three battleships, two cruisers and two destroyers had been sunk or damaged so severely they would be useless for months. Moreover the Supermarina, recoiling from the terrible blow, ordered all major Italian warships to leave Taranto for a safer harbor. Most retired to Naples—too far north to be of much hindrance to the British convoys in the Mediterranean. In effect, the strength of Italy's Navy had been cut in half. All this had been done in just 65 minutes by 21 old-fashioned planes. It proved "once and for all," Admiral Cunningham wrote, "that in the Fleet Air Arm the Navy has its most devastating weapon."

Almost at once, the Taranto strike boosted British fortunes in the North African desert. Cunningham's fleet found it easier to sink Italian supply ships and to shepherd British convoys past Malta to Alexandria, feeding tanks and troops to General Wavell's army. So it was that on December 9, 1940, the beefed-up British ground forces counterattacked the weakened Italian forces and began driving them westward out of Egypt.

"The year 1940 ended in high hope," wrote Cunningham. But the tide of battle had no sooner turned in Britain's favor than it turned again. An old enemy, new to the Mediterranean, appeared: the Germans.

AIRFIELDS AFLOAT

Approaching the carrier Courageous in calm seas, a British Dart prepares for a relatively easy landing in this photograph taken from an escorting warship.

LEARNING TO LAND ON A "BLURRED POSTCARD"

"At 400 feet the deck still looked like a postcard," wrote a British airman of his first landing on an escort carrier. "The stern hurtled toward us. The faces of the handling crew crouching in the side nets rushed up like white cannonballs. My eyes snapped the blurred picture of the control officer crossing his signaling bats for the pilot to cut the engine, and then instantly, as though seized by some giant's hand, we were drawn to a standstill."

That was a typical carrier landing: quick, exciting and successful. But the hazards of landing on a moving airstrip were such that carrier pilots breathed a sigh of relief each time they touched down in one piece. The flight deck offered as little as 100 feet of runway to land on; this meant that the arrester hook under the plane's fuselage had to catch one of the wires stretched across the deck if the plane was to stop without crashing into the safety barriers amidships. The flight deck might rise or fall as much as 65 feet and roll 20 degrees while the pilot made his approach. Yet too much calm was a dangerous thing, for pilots relied on a good head wind to slow their approach.

The biggest problem of all was inexperience. The aircraft carrier was a relatively untried weapon when it was first put to widespread use in the Mediterranean in 1940. Deck-landing was still a new art even for veteran pilots, and the planes they flew were often unsuited to the work. The RAF's Spitfire, for instance, had a long nose that blocked the pilot's view of the deck during landing. But Spitfires were plentiful and planes built for carriers were not. So, as test pilot Eric "Winkle" Brown put it, "the Navy simply stuck an arrester hook on them and played it by ear."

The cost of operating that way could run high. In missions off the coast of southern Italy in 1943, new pilots had to land the speedy Seafires—the Royal Navy's name for Spitfires—on escort carriers about half as long as the regular fleet carriers, and in windless weather. In four days, deck landings claimed 32 planes—results that led British Naval officers to conclude that Seafires should not be used on escort carriers.

A Swordfish (top) approaches the carrier with its hook lowered to snag the arrester wires. The safety barrier looms ahead of the plane at bottom.

A crash-landed Hellcat stands on its nose and the pilot braces himself as the fuselage cracks just aft of the cockpit. The plane fell back right side up.

HAPPY LANDINGS WITH HELP FROM THE DECK

When all went well, deck landings were as routine as newspaper deliveries. The carrier turned into the wind and the landing crew prepared to receive the flight. The first plane began its approach, usually in a gentle, descending curve from the port quarter, and lowered its flaps, wheels and arrester hook. The nose was held high to slow the plane and help the hook catch the arrester wire, and the throttle was held open just enough to prevent a stall.

The pilot watched the wigwagged instructions of the landing control officer, or batsman; the signals told him how to adjust his approach once the plane's nose obscured his view of the flight deck. As soon as the plane, shoulder-high above the deck, crossed the carrier's extreme after end, the batsman brought his bats sharply across his body, meaning "cut the engine." The pilot chopped back the throttle; the plane dropped onto the deck in an abrupt stall and rolled forward until its hook caught one of the arrester wires, the last of which was prayerfully called the for-Christ's-sake wire.

The pilot let the landing crew roll the plane backward a few feet so they could release the wire. Then he taxied over the lowered safety barriers, a pair of steel nets designed to catch planes that missed the wires and thus protect any planes on the forward part of the deck from crashes. The barriers and wires were raised again and the next plane touched down—sometimes only 10 seconds after the first.

A Swordfish torpedo plane approaches the stern of an escort carrier
with its nose up and its tail down while the batsman standing on the deck
stretches out his arms in a signal of approval. The Swordfish's low
stalling speed of 55 knots made it the ideal aircraft for landing on carriers.

A batsman signals an American-made Corsair to cut its engine. In
order to improve his view and reduce his speed, the pilot has banked his
plane toward the carrier, and sideslips to a landing—a typical Corsair
approach. "Every Corsair," observed one pilot, "looked a certain crash."

The aircraft carrier Furious plows up spray in heavy seas, a periodic obstacle to landing planes.

The escort carriers Biter and Avenger battle rough

Holed by German bombs, the Illustrious' flight deck is put temporarily out of use in January 1941.

seas that kept their planes from flying. The Hurricane fighters that were lashed to their decks had fixed wings, which prevented them from being stored below.

WHEN THE SEA TURNED UGLY

"The sea is kind," wrote British pilot Eric Brown, who deck-landed a record 2,407 times. "The airflow is smoother, with no trees, houses, or haystacks to ruffle it." But heavy weather at sea turned an aircraft carrier into a plunging, twisting target. Recalling the near-fatal accident of one fellow pilot who tried to land under such conditions, Brown said the man's plane "was smacked by the after end of the flight deck as it rose and tossed clear above the arrester wires to slither over the port side" into the Mediterranean.

Battle damage to a plane or to the carrier added enormously to the hazards of landing. While a pilot in a crippled plane tried to crash-land, his squadron mates had to wait aloft, their fuel supply dwin-

dling. The bomb damage suffered by the aircraft carrier *Illustrious (opposite, bottom)* off Malta in 1941 was so severe that a number of her planes had to make emergency landings on Malta.

Darkness made every landing problem worse. The control officer, signaling with his illuminated bats or flashlights, often was lost from view in the glow of a Swordfish's red-hot cylinders. Simply finding a blacked-out carrier at night could be terrifying for a pilot. One flier, lost while escorting a convoy to Malta, flashed his navigation lights; the resulting gunfire showed him the position of the carrier. Another pilot landed the same night and sat describing his mission for 20 minutes before he discovered he was not on his own carrier.

Carrier planes were afflicted by a wide assortment of landing mishaps, as these pictures show. The flight-deck crews followed strict priorities: first rescue

the pilots, then spray fire-preventing foam and clear the deck, salvaging whatever could be saved and pushing everything else overboard if necessary.

SURVIVING A CRASH—
"ALL A MATTER OF LUCK"

Deck crashes rarely were fatal, but that knowledge did little to relieve the anxiety of pilots. They knew, as one flier put it, that "some boys were burned to death; some were thrown over the side; others didn't need even an aspirin. It was all a matter of luck."

Even the luckiest had at least a small bureaucratic pain in store: filling out the A25, or accident report. The scarcity of planes and spare parts made it necessary for the pilot to render a strict accounting of any mishap. If a crash aroused the slightest suspicion of carelessness, it was likely to lead to an extremely difficult interview with the ship's captain.

A rescue party on a destroyer carries a pilot to the ship's sick bay for treatment—a hot bath

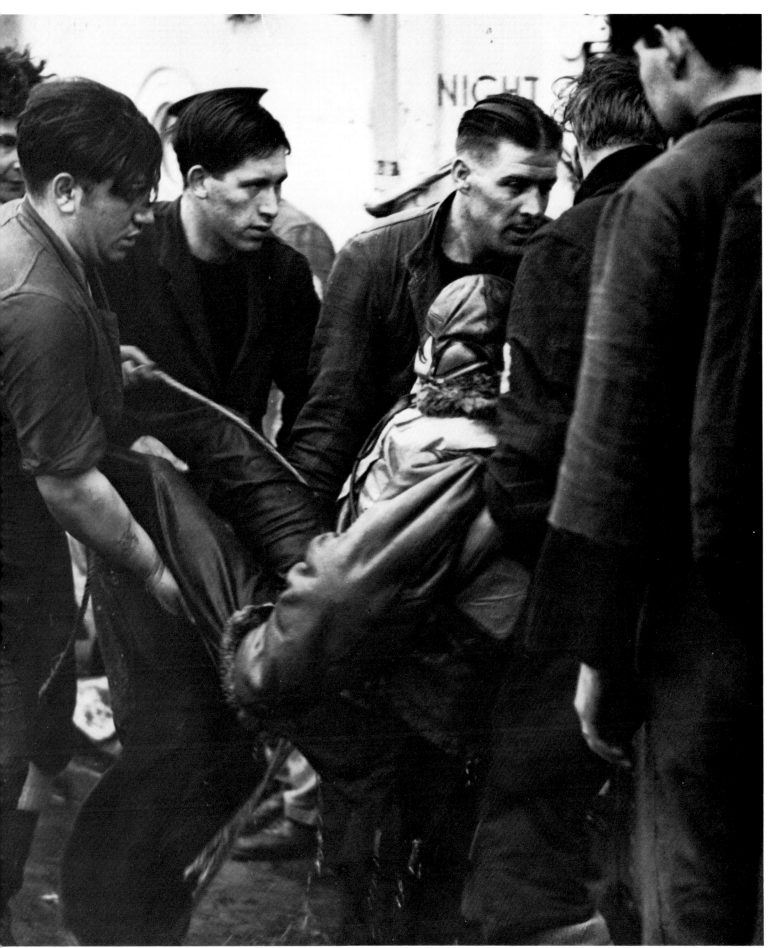

and a warm drink—after plucking him and his gunner from the sea. The airmen had gone overboard when their plane overshot their carrier's flight deck.

3

RETREAT BY SEA

"I am water-shy," Hitler used to tell his aides. "On land I am a lion, but on the water I don't know where to begin." So in late autumn of 1940, after Mussolini had swallowed defeat after defeat on land and the Royal Navy had smashed the Italian fleet at Taranto, threatening to take complete control of the Mediterranean, Hitler responded as an Army man would. *Abschliessen:* Lock it up; close the Mediterranean by capturing its gateway, Gibraltar.

Since this strategy could best be executed by land forces, it hinged on the cooperation of Spain's Francisco Franco, whose country afforded the only land approach to the great fortress. And Franco, who had been tempted earlier in the War to join the Axis to win Gibraltar and large chunks of French North Africa, was now having second thoughts.

Nevertheless, Franco agreed to a meeting with the Führer, and at Hendaye, near Biarritz on the Bay of Biscay, the dictators' private railroad cars came together on the afternoon of October 23, 1940. Franco was an hour late. Sitting in Hitler's plush rail coach, the dour Spaniard listened impassively to Hitler's glowing promises of victory over Britain. The Führer proposed that Spain become a cobelligerent, and that together they attack Gibraltar in January of 1941.

Franco was too clever to say no. Instead he peppered Hitler with challenging questions. England, he pointed out, could be expected to retaliate by blockading Spain's harbors; in that event, would Germany promise to feed Spain? What about the Canary Islands? Might not England seize them, thus establishing another base right off the entrance to the Mediterranean? If the assault did succeed, was Germany prepared to tie down the troops, armaments and warships necessary to hold the base against the expected all-out British counterattack?

After nine hours of conversation, Franco suggested that the matter be discussed further by their Foreign Ministers. Weary and frustrated, Hitler agreed. Later he grumbled to Mussolini that he would rather have three or four teeth pulled than argue with that man again.

Still, the Führer clung to the hope of taking Gibraltar with Franco's aid. Plans for an assault went ahead under the code name Operation *Felix*. But Franco remained as reluctant and as talkative as ever. Finally, in early December, after several days of hemming and hawing in Madrid with Hitler's envoy, Admiral Wilhelm Canaris, Franco said that he could not bring Spain into the War unless England's collapse seemed imminent. And without Spain, there could be no Operation *Felix*.

Stymied on land and unable to contest seriously for the Mediterranean by sea, Hitler turned to the air. On December 10, 1940, he sent several Luftwaffe units to the Mediterranean. One of them was Fliegerkorps X, an elite outfit specially trained to dive-bomb ships. It was transferred to Sicily from Norway, where for months it had been harassing the Royal Navy in the North Sea. Fliegerkorps X was about to make its presence felt in the Mediterranean in combat that would show again—if the British success at Taranto were not proof enough—the devastating effect that air power could have against the most modern warships. In the process, England's Admiral Cunningham would get all the fight he could handle, and a good deal more.

Just after noon on January 10, 1941, Cunningham was standing on the bridge of his flagship, the *Warspite* in the central Mediterranean, supervising the transfer of an eastbound convoy from its Gibraltar escort to the protection of his fleet, when he saw two wave-hopping Italian torpedo bombers heading straight for the nearby aircraft carrier *Illustrious*. All but two of the carrier's Fulmar fighters, which had been circling protectively over the fleet, had landed on her flight deck to refuel. The two airborne Fulmars dived for the enemy planes as the *Illustrious* swung about to dodge the attackers' torpedoes. The Italians climbed and zigzagged away to the northeast, toward Sicily, and the fighters went after them.

From the bridge, Cunningham could see the *Illustrious'* planes revving their engines to take off. At that point he looked up and saw, in faint outline, a wave of planes. They were mere specks in the sky at first, but they came on at great speed. Cunningham guessed that they were flying at about 12,000 feet.

A few moments later he recognized them as German dive bombers, making their first appearance in the Mediterranean theater. There were 36 German planes all told—Stukas and twin-engined Junkers-88s—and their attack was perfectly coordinated. As the *Illustrious'* Fulmars roared off her flight deck and climbed to meet the bombers, the German formation swung over the fleet in a circle. Then half

a dozen broke away to dive toward the *Warspite* and the *Valiant*. The main body of 30 planes concentrated on the *Illustrious*.

The last Fulmar was scarcely in the air when every gun in the British fleet opened up. But the attacking planes came at the *Illustrious* in skillfully orchestrated patterns of evasive action, breaking up into three formations at different altitudes. One formation circled down to about 7,000 feet, rising and dipping to throw off the antiaircraft gunners, then nosed over and came screaming straight at the *Illustrious'* flight deck. Then the other two formations dropped toward the carrier, each from a different direction. The pattern, repeated over and over, was so well executed that the *Illustrious* was constantly under attack by at least six planes.

When they were between 1,200 and 800 feet from the carrier's deck the planes released their bombs. Then, instead of pulling out of their dives, they kept straight on as if they intended to crash, leveling off only at mast-top height and racing the length of the *Illustrious*, spraying her deck with machine-gun fire. From the *Warspite's* bridge Cunningham could see some of the attackers actually flying below the level of the carrier's funnel. While he watched, some of the other planes came snarling over his flagship, and a bomb exploded near the *Warspite's* bow. When Cunningham looked back at the *Illustrious*, he saw the devastating effect of the main attack.

One bomb had sliced through a gun platform on the carrier's forward deck. Another had struck her bow, peeling back the flight deck's armor plating like the top of a sardine can and plunging into her paint locker; even at a distance Cunningham could see the flames and smoke rising from the *Illustrious'* bow. A third bomb had blasted another gun platform loose.

As the attack continued, the damage intensified. A bomb dropped down the carrier's after elevator, demolishing a plane that was being lifted to the deck and blocking the elevator with smoking wreckage. Two minutes later another hit on the same elevator plunged through the tangled steel and exploded inside the hangar. Then another bomb exploded at the top of the forward elevator.

Her interior afire and her steering gear smashed by yet another bomb, the *Illustrious* lurched in an erratic circle. Oozing oily clouds through the craters in her flight deck and spitting flame like a wounded dragon, she wallowed helplessly. That she did not erupt in one mammoth explosion and disappear into the sea was a credit to frantically efficient fire parties.

The entire assault had taken only six and a half minutes. It had taken the carrier's plodding Fulmars that long to climb into position to attack the Germans. But the Germans simply peeled away and fled for Sicily. Cunningham anxiously signaled the *Illustrious,* whose captain, Denis Boyd, replied that he thought he could get the carrier into Malta by using his engines to steer. With the rest of the fleet shepherding her, the smoking vessel headed for port, only to be attacked by more Stukas. This time there were only half as many, and the *Illustrious'* Fulmars, which had flown to Malta and refueled, brought down six of them. The stricken carrier finally reached the shelter of Malta's harbor and its antiaircraft defenses. But it was clear that she would be out of commission for months to come.

The entry of the Luftwaffe into the Mediterranean theater had been dramatic and devastating. "In a few minutes the whole situation had changed," Cunningham recalled. "At one blow the fleet had been deprived of its fighter aircraft, and its command of the Mediterranean was threatened by a weapon far more efficient and dangerous than any against which we had fought before."

The *Illustrious* had been in Malta's harbor barely 12 hours when Fliegerkorps X struck again. The cruisers *Gloucester* and *Southampton,* which had escorted the battle-damaged destroyer *Gallant* to Malta after the first German attack, had set off at top speed to rejoin the rest of the fleet in Alexandria. At 3 p.m. on January 11, a wave of 12 German dive bombers came screaming at them out of the sun.

Both ships were hit, the *Gloucester* by a dud bomb that nevertheless killed nine men and wounded 14 when it hit the bridge dead on. Two bombs struck the *Southampton,* smashing into the petty officers' mess and the wardroom; they killed or crippled nearly all of the ship's senior noncoms and officers, who had been relaxing over an early tea after 48 hours at action stations. The explosions set off a blaze that roared out of control. The survivors abandoned ship and were picked up by the *Gloucester* and a trailing destroyer, the *Diamond.* Finally a British torpedo sent the blazing, listing *Southampton* to the bottom.

Unaccountably, Fliegerkorps X waited six days before attacking the *Illustrious* at Malta, during which time repair crews worked day and night to make the carrier seaworthy enough for an escape run to Alexandria. Some of their work was undone on January 16, when 60 dive bombers plastered the harbor installations and hit the carrier again. During another raid three days later, a bomb that exploded underwater holed the *Illustrious'* hull. Between and after these attacks, technicians and work crews repaired the carrier's

boilers and steering gear, and patched the underwater wound in the hull. But the carrier's flight deck was still a mass of shattered metal, and her elevators were inoperable.

Cunningham dispatched a group of warships from Alexandria to escort the *Illustrious* back. On the 23rd of January, as they made their way west, the ships ran into another Stuka attack. Meanwhile, without waiting for the escort, the blacked-out *Illustrious* slipped out of Malta's harbor unnoticed, leaving her planes behind. She managed 24 knots as she headed for Alexandria, not once making contact with her escort cruisers or with the bombers attacking them.

On January 25, the *Illustrious* steamed into Alexandria harbor. She was out of range of the deadly dive bombers, but she was too crippled to be restored to battle readiness in the Mediterranean. She would have to sail down the Suez Canal, around Africa and—because British shipyards were overcrowded and vulnerable to Luftwaffe attack—across the Atlantic to Norfolk, Virginia, for repairs.

In London, the Admiralty responded to the emergency by sending another modern carrier, the *Formidable*, to Cunningham from her station in the Red Sea. But she had to wait nearly a month for the Suez Canal to be cleared so she could enter the Mediterranean. Meanwhile, Cunningham had only one aircraft carrier available, the outdated *Eagle*, at the very time when the emphasis of the Mediterranean war was changing from surface to air.

After conferring with Mediterranean Air Chief Marshal Sir Arthur Longmore, Cunningham sent an appeal to London for more planes to fight the Germans, and followed it up a few days later with an anguished letter to Admiral Sir Dudley Pound. "There seems to be some bad misunderstanding about the state of our air force out here," Cunningham wrote. "Longmore is absolutely stretched to the limit and we seem to have far fewer planes than is supposed at home." Cunningham and his colleagues estimated the combined German and Italian air strength at 200 dive bombers, bombers and reconnaissance planes—against fewer than 30 British warplanes. Admiral Pound replied that the Battle of the Atlantic was "of supreme importance over all other commitments," but that he would send what few Hurricanes he could spare.

Ironically, British successes in the desert war were making Cunningham's job even more difficult. By the end of

January 1941, General Wavell's army was advancing on Benghazi. The Italian 10th Army had been devastated. But now it was the British whose supply lines were extended, and that meant more convoy duty for Cunningham's fleet along the North African coast, within range of German airfields on Sicily.

No convoy left Alexandria without being spotted by German or Italian reconnaissance planes, and few convoys escaped unscathed from Fliegerkorps X. The minesweeper *Huntley* was sunk on January 31; the gunboat *Terror*, a recent addition to the Inshore Squadron, went down on February 22; the *Dainty*, a destroyer, was lost on February 24; the cruiser *Dorsetshire* was dive-bombed twice and barely made it back to the harbor. At the height of these gantlet-running losses Cunningham heard that he had been made a Knight Grand Cross of the Most Honourable Order of the Bath. He muttered to a friend: "I would sooner have three squadrons of Hurricanes."

The situation worsened. Reacting to the rout of the Italian forces in North Africa, Hitler on February 15 named General Erwin Rommel, an outstanding panzer leader, as commander of the recently formed Afrika Korps. And to make sure that Germany's entry into the North Africa campaign would not be impeded, Fliegerkorps X was instructed to neutralize Malta.

From January through April of 1941, high-altitude bomb-

Adolf Hitler and Spain's Francisco Franco pass a German honor guard during their meeting on the French-Spanish border in October of 1940. Franco resisted Hitler's pressure to join in the war against England.

A German airman stationed in Sicily shaves using a prickly-pear cactus to hang his mirror and his clothes. The members of Fliegerkorps X welcomed the balmy Sicilian climate following a tour of duty in Norway.

ers unleashed avalanches of destruction on the island, their raids interspersed with shrieking attacks by dive-bombing Stukas. In these raids, the Luftwaffe lost 60 planes to the spunky defense of Malta's few Hurricanes and the Fulmars left behind by the *Illustrious*. But the unremitting raids achieved their purpose: Only four surface ships made it to Malta during the four-month-long air barrage. A few submarines, lurking underwater during the raids and sneaking out at night, managed to hit several Axis convoys ferrying the Afrika Korps to Tripoli.

The raids on Malta did not let up until the end of May, when most of Fliegerkorps X was ordered to North Africa to support Rommel. Meanwhile, Hitler once again had been forced to come to the aid of Mussolini, this time in Greece.

The Italian invasion of Greece, which began on October 28, 1940, had lasted less than a month. The Italian tanks bogged down in the mountainous terrain, and sure-footed Greek soldiers, some dragging artillery over craggy trails too narrow and steep even for mules, stopped the invaders and drove them back into Albania, where desultory fighting continued. The Greek government declined to ask Great Britain for ground troops, but it permitted the British to build several air bases in Greece and to establish a naval base at Suda Bay on Crete to protect supply convoys to Greece.

By the spring of 1941, Hitler was busily preparing his invasion of the Soviet Union. In order to guard his southern flank for that momentous assault, he laid emergency plans to rescue Mussolini's fortunes in Greece and also to liquidate an alarming anti-German coup d'étât in Yugoslavia. But Hitler's orders for the Balkan invasion were deciphered by the British radio-decoding operation named *Ultra,* and Churchill finally persuaded the Greek government to accept British troops.

As soldiers from all over the Commonwealth poured into Greece during March, Hitler decided to find out if Mussolini's navy could be counted on, since his army could not. Ever since the *Illustrious'* torpedo bombers had crippled the Italian fleet in Taranto, Italy's admirals had been loath to engage Cunningham's ships. Now the Germans urged their reluctant partners to attack the British convoys to Greece.

Admiral Arturo Riccardi, Italy's Naval Chief of Staff, demurred and delayed, arguing that such an action would take his ships too far from home and that British reconnaissance planes from Crete and Alexandria would deprive them of the element of surprise. What is more, his fleet needed fuel. But at the Germans' insistence, and with their promise of air cover for the Italian fleet, the Duce ordered Riccardi to attack Cunningham's fleet, and Riccardi bucked the order down to Mediterranean Commander in Chief Admiral Angelo Iachino. The stage was being set for a hectic, sprawling battle off Greece's Cape Matapan—the nearest thing to a classic naval battle fought during the Mediterranean war.

The setting for the battle of Matapan was completed by some weighty deception on the part of Cunningham. On March 27, 1941, Cunningham was alerted by *Ultra* that the Italian fleet was steaming into the Aegean. To protect his top-secret intelligence source, he sent out a flying boat that passed close enough to spot the Italians—and, in turn, to be spotted by them. Cunningham assumed that the Italians knew about and would try to wipe out a small British convoy that was making way through the Aegean to Greece. He also assumed that the Italian fleet would back off if the departure of his own warships was reported by the chief Axis spy in Alexandria, the Japanese consul general. This official was a pear-shaped figure whom a local wag described as "the blunt end of the Axis." He was a devoted golfer.

Cunningham ordered the fleet to get up steam. Then, to deceive the Japanese consul, he ostentatiously appeared at the golf club prepared to stay overnight. Predictably, the Japanese consul was at the club, and Cunningham made sure he was observed by the diplomat-spy. Then the admiral slipped back on board the *Warspite*. That night the 13-ship fleet, which included the carrier *Formidable*, three battleships and nine destroyers, sailed under cover of darkness.

A mishap occurred even before Cunningham was out of the harbor: The *Warspite* passed too close to a mudbank and clogged her condensers. Once all the ships were at sea and heading north northwest, it was discovered that the fouled condensers had reduced the *Warspite's* top speed from 24 knots to about 20 knots. At that speed, the fleet steamed through the night toward the unsuspecting Italians.

Meanwhile, the commander of the small Naval force escorting the convoy, Vice Admiral H. D. Pridham-Wippell, was playing his part in the cat-and-mouse game. He had continued toward Piraeus until dark; then, leaving a few

German bombers pummel Malta's Grand Harbor in January of 1941. The bomb smoke and geysers of water at right obscure the aircraft carrier Illustrious, *which had sought shelter in the harbor after suffering heavy damage during repeated onslaughts by 130 Luftwaffe bombers.*

warships to escort the troopships, he reversed course to join forces with Cunningham southwest of Gavdos Island and to seek out the Italians.

Though it included no aircraft carriers, the Italian fleet they were after was a powerful one, the largest to put to sea since the British attack on Taranto. Admiral Iachino flew his flag aboard the modern battleship *Vittorio Veneto,* which was supported by six heavy cruisers, two light cruisers and more than a dozen destroyers.

Pacing the bridge of the *Warspite* in what his staff called his "caged-tiger act," Cunningham walked miles back and forth as if willing his balky flagship to greater speed to catch the elusive Italians. Before sailing from Alexandria he had made a bet of 10 shillings with his Operations Staff Officer, Commander Manley Power, that this would be a futile chase. But at 7:40 a.m., Pridham-Wippell's flagship, the cruiser *Orion,* radioed that she had sighted three enemy ships north of her position. "I cheerfully paid up my 10 shillings," Cunningham recalled.

Pridham-Wippell's eight ships—four cruisers and four

destroyers—were still about 90 miles northwest of Cunningham, and the Italian ships were closing on them quickly. As they came nearer, Pridham-Wippell could see that they were heavy cruisers that could easily outgun him.

By 8:12 a.m., the Italians had come within 13 miles of Pridham-Wippell, and they opened fire with their 8-inch guns. The shells straddled the British cruiser *Gloucester,* which zigzagged to avoid being hit. When the range was down to 12 miles, the *Gloucester* returned fire but the shells from her 6-inch guns fell far short of her pursuers. However, this show of defiance gave the Italians pause; they swung westward and ceased fire.

Pridham-Wippell also took his force westward, trying to keep out of range but in sight, hoping to entice the Italian cruisers to follow him right into Cunningham's big guns. For two hours he kept up this game—and then discovered his mistake. Instead of luring the enemy cruisers toward his battleships, he himself had been duped: There on the northern horizon, steaming down on his cruisers at 30 knots, was the battleship *Vittorio Veneto.*

At a range of 16 miles, the Italians opened fire. Pridham-Wippell turned and ran for the protection of Cunningham's fleet, radioing a call for help and sending a smoke screen astern. As he ran, huge geysers from near misses by the *Vittorio Veneto's* 15-inch shells splashed all around him.

Still some 50 miles away, Cunningham was faced with a dilemma: If he sent immediate help to Pridham-Wippell, he might scare off the enemy. On the other hand, if he delayed,

he might lose all of Pridham-Wippell's cruisers. Cunningham gave the order to the battleship *Valiant:* Get up full speed (24 knots) and go to the rescue. And to the *Formidable,* whose planes were already circling in the air, he signaled: Go get them.

Shortly, the torpedo planes were diving at the Italian battleship and her escorting cruisers and destroyers. Now the Italians were forced to turn their energies to repelling the planes, and Pridham-Wippell got away. Even the *Gloucester,* which had had engine trouble and was making less than full speed, escaped. "The sight of an enemy battleship," Cunningham noted sarcastically, "somehow increased the *Gloucester's* speed to 30 knots."

To supply similar inspiration aboard the mud-clogged *Warspite,* Cunningham summoned Engineer Captain B. J. H. Wilkinson to the bridge. Recalled Cunningham, "I told him to do something about it"—no doubt using more vivid language. Shortly the *Warspite* was picking up speed and even keeping pace with the *Valiant* as she charged northwest toward the Italians. The *Formidable* could not keep pace with the cruisers; she had to turn into the wind each time she launched or retrieved her planes, and the wind was from the northeast.

The pilots of the *Formidable's* first returning flight radioed that they had hit a battleship, which they believed to be the *Vittorio Veneto.* A jumble of reports came crackling in from the planes: Two more enemy battleships, accompanied by 8-inch cruisers, and another force of cruisers were all

speeding westward, getting away as fast as they could.

It was 12:30 p.m. when Pridham-Wippell finally joined Cunningham's force in pursuit of the Italians. At the time, the *Vittorio Veneto* and her escort were reported 65 miles to the west. At 3 p.m. an RAF flying boat placed her still 65 miles ahead of the fleet. Clearly, the torpedo attack had not slowed her enough for the British fleet to catch up with her. A second wave of torpedo planes was sent out and returned with a report that the battleship had been hit again and that her speed was down to eight knots.

The hit had been made by Lieut. Commander J. Dalyell-Stead, who demonstrated what the captain of the *Vittorio Veneto* called "the greatest skill and highest courage": He put his torpedo into the battleship's stern before he was shot down while attempting to pull out of his dive. But at 4 p.m. came the news from an RAF reconnaissance plane that the *Vittorio Veneto* had increased her speed to 12 to 15 knots despite the torpedo damage. It now looked as though she would escape as darkness came on.

Chafing with frustration, Cunningham ordered a search plane catapulted from the *Warspite,* and he sent Pridham-Wippell's *Orion* and three other cruisers on ahead. It was 6:30 p.m. before the plane radioed that the *Vittorio Veneto* and her escort were now 55 miles away, still steaming westward. Cunningham ordered a final torpedo-plane strike at dusk. By the time these planes returned, reporting only "probable" hits, it was 7:30 and nearly dark.

Cunningham now faced the most difficult decision of the battle: whether or not to engage the enemy at night. As he paced the charthouse deck, circling the chalk-marked enemy formation, his aides gave their opinions. Most of them argued against pursuit at night: The enemy force outnumbered the British, it could change course while Cunningham plunged blindly ahead, its blacked-out ships could not be seen from the *Formidable's* planes, and they were beyond the 12,000-yard range of the few British radar sets. Even if the Italians could be brought into action, one argument went, there was the risk of firing on British ships in a melee at night. Not since the Battle of the Nile in 1798 had a nighttime naval battle been decisive, and even then Nelson had attacked before dark.

Still, Cunningham refused to give up a prize as great as the *Vittorio Veneto.* He listened to the objections and snapped, "You're a pack of yellow-livered skunks! I'll go and have my supper now and see after supper if my morale isn't higher than yours." It had been a long and difficult day.

Cunningham returned from his dinner with a plan of attack. His speedy destroyers would race ahead to the west at their top speed of 36 knots and establish contact with the enemy, signaling to the British cruisers as they came on. Meanwhile, Cunningham would take his battleships and the *Formidable* northwest. If the Italians changed course, he reasoned, they would probably head northwest toward Taranto—and he could cut them off.

Pridham-Wippell was still out ahead with his four cruisers, hoping to pick up the enemy formation on his one radar set. At 9:11 p.m. a large blip flickered onto the screen: A ship lay dead in the water about five miles away. Was she the *Vittorio Veneto?* Had the dusk raid succeeded after all? If so, it seemed unlikely that the rest of the Italian fleet would have deserted a capital ship. Pridham-Wippell radioed Cunningham of his sighting and kept on his course westward. Cunningham ordered a change of course. He would look into this before turning northwest.

The *Warspite* had not yet been fitted with radar, but the *Valiant* had, and her screen soon picked up the stranger six miles away. "She was a large ship," Cunningham recalled. "The *Valiant* gave her length as 600 feet." He ordered another course change of 40 degrees to close on her. "Action Stations" sounded through the intercoms. Gun crews locked onto the enemy ship's compass bearing.

Six hundred feet was battleship length; she could indeed be the *Vittorio Veneto.* But she was not. She was the heavy cruiser *Pola,* torpedoed and crippled during the carrier planes' last attack. As Cunningham moved in on the *Pola,* an Italian force was coming to her rescue, as yet unnoticed by the *Valiant's* radar.

It was 10:25 p.m. A light mist hid the stars and reduced visibility to about two miles. The enemy ship should have been right off the *Warspite's* port bow. Every man on the bridge was straining to see through his binoculars, searching the dark horizon to port. Commander John Edelsten, Cunningham's chief of staff, went to the starboard side to sweep the horizon—and caught his breath. His binoculars swinging on their strap, he walked quickly across the bridge

The Royal Navy light cruisers Ajax and Perth, under attack by the Italian battleship Vittorio Veneto, belch protective screens of black smoke from their funnels and white smoke from chemical pots on their sterns at the beginning of the battle of Matapan. The cruiser Gloucester, from whose deck this picture was taken, was situated too far to the windward to be concealed by the smoke screen and soon came under heavy attack.

to Cunningham. Softly, almost as if afraid to be heard across the water, Edelsten reported what he had seen: two large cruisers, with a smaller ship ahead of them, lying off the *Warspite's* starboard bow.

Commander Manley Power, an ex-submariner whom Cunningham considered "an abnormal expert at recognizing the silhouettes of enemy warships at a glance," studied the dark shapes barely outlined on the horizon and pronounced them to be two 8-inch cruisers, led by a smaller cruiser. (The third ship actually was the *Alfieri,* a destroyer.) Evidently unaware of the danger, the Italian ships were moving on a converging course with the British ships.

Here were the juiciest targets Cunningham had encountered in nearly a year. Signaling through a special short-range radio, he turned his fleet into the classic line-ahead formation—all ships stationed to present their combined broadsides to the oncoming cruisers. As the unsuspecting Italians converged on the British line of battle, Cunningham ran up the steel ladder to the upper bridge, followed by his

aides. From here they had a commanding 360-degree view.

"I shall never forget the next few minutes," Cunningham later wrote. "In the dead silence, a silence that could almost be felt, one heard only the voices of the gun-control personnel putting the guns onto the new target. One heard the orders repeated in the director tower behind and above the bridge. Looking forward, one saw the turrets swing and steady when the 15-inch guns pointed at the enemy cruisers." On the ships came, their captains unaware that an entire British fleet was waiting to blow them out of the water.

The Italian ships were so close that their bow waves could be made out through binoculars. Behind him, Cunningham heard a voice in the director tower announce softly: "Director layer sees target." That meant the *Warspite's* mighty guns were homed in at a range of no more than 3,800 yards—point blank.

Fleet Gunnery Officer Geoffrey Barnard ordered the ships to open fire. Through the intercom sounded the *ting-ting-ting* of the firing gongs. The *Warspite* shuddered as an en-

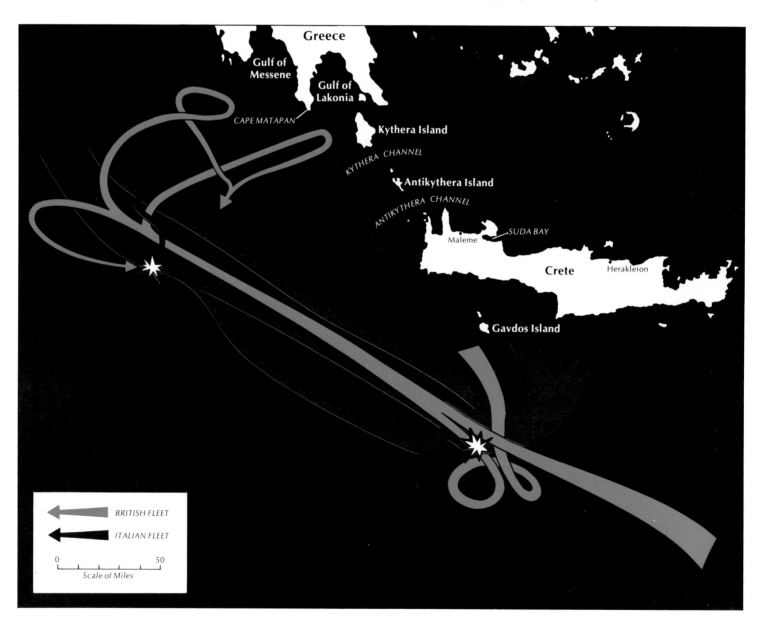

veloping orange flash erupted from her side. Six huge guns had let go at once.

At the same time, the searchlights went on. From the bridge, Cunningham saw the silver-blue shape of a cruiser spring out of the darkness. He could even track the flight of the *Warspite's* first salvo, six shells arcing across the black water and directly into the cruiser. Five of them smashed into the side of the ship just below its upper deck. There was a flashing explosion. The *Warspite's* gunnery officer exclaimed, "Good Lord! We've hit her!"

Cunningham swung his binoculars to the other cruiser. The *Valiant* had fired at the same instant, with the same result. The second cruiser exploded as if an enormous bomb had gone off inside her. Then the destroyer *Greyhound* caught the *Alfieri* in her spotlights and hit her with a broadside at 3,100 yards. As Cunningham watched, the *Warspite*, *Valiant* and the battleship *Barham* repeated their rapid-fire broadsides. The Italian ships, their guns still aimed fore and aft, were hit repeatedly before they could fire a shot. Whole gun turrets flew into the air. Showers of hot metal splashed hissing into the sea. The sky was lit up by flames.

In the course of only a few minutes the *Warspite* had slammed two broadsides of 15-inch shells—each shell nearly a ton of hurtling metal—into the first cruiser, the *Fiume,* and four into the second, the *Zara.* The *Valiant* had sent one broadside into the *Fiume* and five into the *Zara,* which also had been hit by six broadsides from the *Barham.* The big cruisers were quickly reduced to burning hulks, while the water swarmed with men who had dived overboard. The *Alfieri,* listing heavily to starboard, escaped under a smoke screen; she was hit again later and sank.

As the British fleet's starboard guns pounded the cruisers, three enemy destroyers appeared on the port side. One launched a cluster of torpedoes, whose tracks were spotted in time for the British to evade them with a 90-degree turn. The battleships drove the Italian destroyers off, and one of them, the *Carducci,* was sunk by a torpedo from the British destroyer *Havock.* In the ensuing confusion, one of the *Warspite's* searchlights picked out an ominous shape about five miles to starboard. The British signal officer quickly called the bearing to the gunnery officer: "Green 60, enemy cruiser!" Cunningham took one look and said, "Don't be a bloody idiot! It's the *Formidable.*" The order was counter-manded just as the *Warspite's* guns were homing in on her own late-arriving carrier.

Cunningham took his battleships off to join the *Formidable,* and sent four destroyers in to finish off the burning Italian cruisers. Then came a succession of British mistakes. Pridham-Wippell, still chasing the *Vittorio Veneto,* intercepted Cunningham's signal to his battleships to regroup, and apparently took it to indicate that the ship he had spotted on his radar had been the *Vittorio Veneto* after all and that she had been caught. He broke off his chase and steamed back to rejoin the fleet.

Then about midnight, the British destroyer *Havock* repeated the mistake Cunningham had made earlier: She came upon the big Italian cruiser *Pola,* still sitting dead in the water, and reported having sighted an enemy battleship. The report reached the British destroyers that, along with Pridham-Wippell, had been chasing the *Vittorio Veneto.* The destroyers' commander, Captain Philip Mack, believed that he had passed his prey, and turned back. Actually, the *Vittorio Veneto* was only 30 miles from Mack, and she was moving ever closer to the safety of Taranto.

By the time Mack's destroyers came across the *Pola,* it was 3 a.m. on March 29. The *Pola* had been wallowing in the Aegean, her engines out of commission, for six hours. After she had been torpedoed, her sailors had abandoned her, ceremoniously saluting, then stripping and diving overboard. But the *Pola* did not sink, so about a quarter of the ship's 1,000-man company had swum back and climbed on board. Then, unaware of the confusion their cruiser was causing, the shivering crew broke into the officers' liquor supply and got helplessly drunk.

Mack sent his gun crews—some of whom were armed for the occasion with cutlasses as well as Sten guns—to board the *Pola.* The Italian ship was in a riotous state. Many of her crewmen were still naked from their brief swim; stumbling, singing and vomiting, they were herded on board the British destroyer *Jervis.* At 4:10 a.m., a final torpedo slammed into the *Pola's* side, and the battle of Matapan ended as the ship sank in a giant, oily bubble.

Dawn found the reassembled British fleet moving slowly through wreckage, rafts, lifeboats and corpses, picking up survivors from the *Zara* and *Fiume.* Some 900 men were

A succession of searches and chases, the battle of Matapan sprawled over 290 miles. The first clash between the British (blue) and Italian forces (red) occurred about 60 miles south of Crete on the morning of March 28, 1941. In the last action, the Italians, led by the battleship Vittorio Veneto, were fleeing northwestward when the British caught up with a part of their fleet and attacked at night, sinking three cruisers and two destroyers.

rescued before the drone of German Ju-88s warned the British off. The sea was still dotted with swimmers, so Cunningham radioed their position to the Italian Admiralty. An Italian hospital ship steamed to the area in time to save 160 more men, and a flotilla of Greek destroyers rescued another 110 sailors.

In the final reckoning, the battle casualties were wildly disproportionate. Three of Italy's biggest cruisers and two destroyers had been sunk in the battle of Matapan, with an estimated loss of 2,400 men. The British loss: one torpedo plane and its crew of three. As Nelson had done after his nighttime victory at the Nile, Cunningham ordered a special thanksgiving service held on all his ships on April 1, the day after their safe return to Alexandria.

There was no rest for Cunningham's victorious fleet. In early April, even as German armies plunged into Yugoslavia and Greece, his warships pounded the Libyan coast, searched for Libya-bound Italian supply ships, and escorted British troopships and supply convoys from Alexandria to Greece. In addition, units of the fleet sowed mines in Benghazi harbor, attacked enemy airfields on the island of Rhodes, and ran errands to and from beleaguered Malta. Cunningham was also assigned a mission that he felt—and argued—would be less risky for the RAF: to wreck Tripoli, the most important Axis supply terminus in Libya.

Cunningham lost the argument, and on April 18 he left Alexandria with three battleships, two cruisers, the carrier *Formidable* and a screen of nine destroyers. Shortly before dawn on April 21 the fleet was in position four miles off Tripoli, its presence apparently undetected by the Italian shore batteries.

At 5 a.m. the British guns opened up on the port and its oil-storage tanks. It took the startled Italians 20 minutes to respond to the British bombardment—and their return fire scored not a single hit. At 5:45 a.m. Cunningham withdrew, having shelled the harbor into a flaming pyre. He was amazed by the fleet's good luck. "My personal fears had ranged from the complete loss of a ship in a minefield," Cunningham later wrote, "to heavy damage to them all by dive bombing. We had been incredibly fortunate." He added with asperity, however: "It had taken the whole Mediterranean fleet five days to accomplish what a heavy-bomber squadron working from Egypt could probably have carried out in a few hours."

While Cunningham and his ships were returning to Alexandria, the Germans were mauling the British expeditionary force in Greece. It became clear that only Cunningham's ships could save them.

Cunningham would have to pull off another Dunkirk, this time with the enemy in full command of the air. The Luftwaffe vastly outnumbered the RAF in Greece, and as the British troops there gave ground, the British planes were flown to Crete and the airfields were left to the Germans. The carrier planes of the *Formidable* would have to provide practically all the air cover for ships sent to pick up the fleeing British soldiers.

Back in Alexandria, Cunningham quickly worked out the

details of the rescue operation. Half a dozen beaches along the southern coast of Greece were selected for the evacuations, which were to take place late at night to avoid the German dive bombers expected with the dawn.

The first evacuation took place on April 24, four days ahead of schedule; the Germans were coming on too quickly to allow for a more leisurely withdrawal. Blacked-out British cruisers and destroyers moved along the coastline and sent in their boats, safely taking off more than 12,000 men at Raphti and Nauplia. For five more harrowing nights the ships repeated their performance. Nearly 6,000 men, many of them wounded, were rescued from Megara on the second night. The third evacuation was the most successful: 21,000 men were ferried away from five beaches during one night. On the fourth night, as the Germans were marching unopposed into Athens, 4,600 more men got away, and on the fifth night 5,000 more escaped.

By May 1, the evacuation was over. Nearly 50,000 British, Commonwealth and Greek soldiers had been rescued. Some 11,000 were left behind. Of these, a few hundred stragglers eventually made their way, in an assortment of leaky Greek sailing ships, across the 50 miles of open Aegean to Greece's southernmost island, Crete.

Crete was a welcome haven for the battered troops who had fled from Greece. But the island was a refuge only briefly. On the morning of May 20 the Germans launched Operation *Mercury,* a great airborne assault against Crete, involving 13,000 parachutists and glider troops, and 9,000 mountain troops brought in by Ju-52 transports.

British ground forces battled the Germans on Crete's airstrips and open fields, managing to contain much of the first wave. Meanwhile, Cunningham was assigned to prevent German waterborne reinforcements and heavy ordnance from reaching the island. The task was dangerous in the extreme. The Luftwaffe controlled the skies; the nearest RAF fighters were based in Egypt and could cover only the western tip of the island. Furthermore, all but four of the *Formidable's* planes had been put out of action during a convoy patrol. Cunningham's ships would have no protection save their own antiaircraft guns.

To avoid the Luftwaffe as much as possible, Cunningham decided to patrol Crete's northern coast by night and, barring reports of approaching enemy convoys, to withdraw his ships by day to the relative safety of the southern coast. Three groups of destroyers and cruisers were to make the patrols; the rest of the fleet would be held in reserve at Alexandria, where Cunningham would direct operations.

At dawn on the 21st of May, the second day of the attack, German aircraft drew first blood. They sank the British destroyer *Juno* and damaged the cruiser *Ajax,* which were returning from a bombardment of the Luftwaffe base on the island of Scarpanto, 50 miles east of Crete. Then the serious fighting started.

That afternoon, near the island of Milos, an RAF reconnaissance plane spied a large enemy flotilla of destroyers and caïques—twin-masted wooden motor sailers. Alerted by the RAF report, Rear Admiral I. G. Glennie set out with seven warships to lie in wait for the German force, timing his journey to arrive in the bomber-haunted waters north of Suda Bay just after dark.

A few minutes before midnight, the first seaborne German landing force was sighted: a flotilla of caïques carrying an estimated 2,300 troops and escorted by an Italian destroyer, the *Lupo.* For the next two hours, the *Lupo's* commander defiantly and uselessly charged the British destroyers. The *Lupo* was finally driven off—after taking no fewer than eighteen 6-inch shells—and 10 caïques were sunk, carrying about 800 Germans to their deaths in the Aegean. The rest of the caïques fled for Greece. Of the entire landing force, only 49 men in life rafts made it ashore on Crete.

Meanwhile, Rear Admiral Edward L. S. King had taken his group of ships north of Herakleion to look for more seaborne invaders. At 8:30 a.m. on May 22 a flotilla of caïques appeared on the horizon—this time supported by Luftwaffe dive bombers. Despite nearly constant air attack, King managed to sink one troop-carrying caïque and to drive the others back toward Greece. By 10 a.m., with his antiaircraft ammunition nearly gone, King prudently turned his ships south and ran for his life.

The German airmen took a heavy toll on the fleeing ships. They sank the destroyer *Greyhound,* damaged two more de-

A rowboat ferries a party of RAF airmen to a Sunderland flying boat during the British evacuation of Greece in April 1941. Among the countless civilian craft that were pressed into service was a motorboat that carried six airmen and two nuns from Athens to Alexandria, 600 miles distant.

King George II of Greece (left) and Second Lieutenant W. H. Ryan relax after escaping from Crete in May 1941. Ryan's platoon had escorted the King on a three-day trek across the island's mountainous western end to a southern coastal village, where a British destroyer picked them up.

stroyers and smashed half of the *Warspite's* antiaircraft guns. The cruiser *Gloucester* had to be left dead in the water; it later sank.

The cruiser *Fiji,* her ammunition expended, was reduced to firing practice shells at the bombers that snarled over her as she picked up survivors from the *Greyhound.* The *Fiji* held out against countless bombing attacks before falling victim to a lone Me-109 fighter. The pilot dived out of a hazy sky and released a single 500-pound bomb, which hit the *Fiji* amidships. The explosion holed the bottom of the cruiser; she immediately heeled over to port at a 25-degree list, her engines crippled. Within half an hour, another plane dropped three bombs that struck the *Fiji.* These blows were fatal, and the crew abandoned ship. An hour later, the cruiser rolled over and sank.

That night two destroyers slipped back and rescued 523 men from the *Fiji.* One survivor, who had been rescued earlier from the *Greyhound,* reported that the dive bombers had strafed the crewmen in his lifeboat; he dived into the water and came up to find everyone in the lifeboat dead.

Admiral King had suffered terrible losses, but he had given the British ground forces on Crete a breathing space. The German troop-transport commander, seeing his caïques driven back, canceled the departure of a larger force, carrying not only 4,000 troops but much-needed tanks as well.

British Naval losses continued to rise. The next day, May 23, a group of destroyers from Malta under Captain Lord Louis Mountbatten sank some troop-carrying caïques north of Maleme, and was attacked in turn by 24 Stukas. The destroyer *Kashmir* was sunk, and a succession of bomb hits mortally wounded Mountbatten's destroyer, the *Kelly.*

The crew of the *Kelly* began to abandon ship. In minutes, she turned turtle, trapping the engineering officer, Commander Michael Evans, and three of his men inside the flooded engine room. They all bobbed up into a giant air bubble. Each man sucked a lungful of air, groped down steel ladders, swam out a hatch and shot toward the surface.

Evans and two of his men made it; they found many fellow survivors on the surface, including Mountbatten, who was nearly blinded from swimming through an oil slick. The men were soon picked up by the destroyer *Kipling.* With Stukas screaming overhead, the *Kipling* raced to and fro on her rescue mission. Somehow she emerged unscathed and reached Alexandria carrying 279 survivors from the *Kelly.* (Mountbatten later told the story of his rescue to playwright Noel Coward, who dramatized the episode in the film *In Which We Serve.*)

Nearly every report from the fleet to Cunningham in Alexandria brought news of similar losses. "I came to dread every ring of the telephone, every knock on the door, and the arrival of every fresh signal," Cunningham wrote. One message was particularly painful: First Lieutenant Walter Starkie, the husband of his niece Hilda, who was living with the Cunninghams, had gone down with his destroyer.

For the British, the news from Crete went from depressing to desperate. By May 21, within 24 hours of the attack on Crete, the Germans had won complete control of the Maleme airfield on the island's northwest coast, enabling wave after wave of transport planes to inundate the island with fresh troops and supplies. The British ground forces had no choice but to retreat over Crete's mountainous spine, all the while radioing Alexandria for reinforcements. From London came Churchill's impassioned appeal: "Crete must be won. Fighting must be maintained indefinitely."

Cunningham responded to the best of his limited capacity. "Stick it out," he exhorted the fleet. "Navy must not let Army down. No enemy forces must reach Crete by sea." On the afternoon of May 23 he sent the cruiser *Coventry,* the assault ship *Glenroy* and a small supply convoy toward Suda Bay, 13 miles from Maleme Field. But German air activity was so intense that Cunningham ordered the *Coventry* and her charges to turn back later that evening. "It appeared to be sheer murder to send her on," he recalled.

To Cunningham's astonishment, the Admiralty in London countermanded his order and sent the *Coventry* back toward Crete. Cunningham immediately turned tough with his superiors. Countermanding the Admiralty's order, he told London that if the convoy continued toward Crete, it would surely fall victim to the Luftwaffe's morning attacks. "The less said about this unjustifiable interference by those ignorant of the situation," he said sharply, "the better."

To relieve the pressure on his fleet, Cunningham mounted another attack on the Luftwaffe base on Scarpanto. He sent the *Formidable,* which had scraped up 12 fighter planes, escorted by the battleships *Queen Elizabeth* and

BRIEF UNION OF A VALIANT PAIR

When Captain Lord Louis Mountbatten assumed command of the Royal Navy's aircraft carrier *Illustrious* in August 1941, the union of man and ship seemed singularly appropriate. Both were battle-singed veterans of the war in the Mediterranean: Mountbatten's destroyer, the *Kelly*, had been sunk beneath him off Crete, and the *Illustrious* had been severely damaged by Axis warplanes off Malta.

As it turned out, however, Mountbatten never took his new command to sea. While the carrier was being overhauled in a shipyard in the United States, Prime Minister Churchill selected Mountbatten to direct Combined Operations, an organization charged with executing commando raids in German-occupied Europe—and using that experience to plan major assaults combining sea, land and air forces.

Mountbatten, an inveterate sailor, tried to turn Churchill down. But when Churchill truculently asked what he could possibly hope to accomplish with the *Illustrious* "except to be sunk in a bigger and more expensive ship," Mountbatten accepted the Combined Operations command. He became, in Churchill's newly coined phrase, "a complete triphibian—a creature equally at home in earth, air and water, and also well accustomed to fire."

The *Illustrious*, under a new skipper, made her own contribution to Combined Operations. The carrier provided air cover for the 1942 British landings in Madagascar, the first large-scale triphibian operation, and the next year played a key part in the successful Allied invasion of Italy.

Lord Mountbatten stands on the bridge of the Kelly before its sinking. Said a crewman: "We'd paddle Lord Louis up the Rhine on a raft."

British sailors and Marines look on as Mountbatten takes command of the Illustrious at Norfolk, Virginia, where the ship was undergoing major repairs.

Barham and eight destroyers. At dawn on May 26 the force's commander, Pridham-Wippell, ordered the *Formidable* to launch her planes. Four Albacores and four Fulmars reached Scarpanto undetected, destroyed two aircraft on the ground and damaged a few others. But the British would pay dearly for that assault.

Several hours later, a German attack group of 20 bombers spotted the *Formidable* and her escort. As the carrier turned into the wind to launch her planes, she was hit twice: One bomb blew out a forward section of her hull, the second damaged one of her gun turrets and her steering cable. Another German bomb hit the destroyer *Nubian,* shattering her stern. Screened by four destroyers, the *Formidable* and the *Nubian* limped toward Alexandria.

At the same time, Cunningham was holding a council of war in Alexandria with General Wavell, Air Chief Marshal Arthur Tedder, the new RAF commander in the area, General Sir Thomas Blamey, commander of Australia's Middle East forces, and Peter Fraser, Prime Minister of New Zealand, who was visiting the area because many of his troops were fighting on Crete. Despite exhortations from Churchill to "keep hurling in all you can," the main topic of the meeting was evacuation.

Could the fleet do it? How could it penetrate the Germans' curtain of fire to bring out the troops? Already the battle for Crete had put two battleships, a carrier, three cruisers and five destroyers out of action; five more cruisers and four destroyers were so badly damaged that they might not be repaired in time to help. Still, Cunningham insisted that it was unthinkable to abandon the troops in Crete. "It takes the Navy three years to build a ship," he told aides. "It would take three hundred to rebuild a tradition."

On the night of May 28, a little more than 24 hours after the decision to evacuate, four destroyers nosed up to the wharves of Sphakia, on the southwest coast of Crete, and steamed south with the first 700 men. Over the next three nights, 12,000 men were evacuated from Sphakia. So efficiently did the operation proceed that the Luftwaffe, which had no night fighters, had only a few daylight hours in which to attack. And in that period the RAF, which could cover Sphakia from North African bases, managed to keep the Germans at bay.

A more dangerous mission was the evacuation of Herakleion on the northern side of the island—beyond the RAF's range. The rescue force of three cruisers and six destroyers would have to shoot the gap of Kasos Strait in daylight on the run up and again on the return to Alexandria, presenting a tempting target for German fighters on Scarpanto.

At 5 p.m. on May 28 the Germans appeared as expected, and along with them Italian bombers and torpedo planes. The raiders subjected the British warships to a steady stream of dive-bombing and torpedo runs until darkness fell. The cruiser *Ajax* was damaged by a near-miss explosion that started a fire and wounded 20 men, forcing the ship to turn back to Alexandria. Another bomb exploded near the destroyer *Imperial's* steering gear; she appeared undamaged and steamed on to Herakleion.

There, the cruisers slowed while the blacked-out destroyers moved up to the jetty. "Like a wraith we crept into the northern wall," recalled an officer on board one of the destroyers. "We got in alongside with a minimum of light and noise, no one raising his voice to a shout, as the Germans were pretty close to the harbor."

More than 4,000 tired troops quickly filed aboard the destroyers. Several who had gone out on the wrong jetty wasted no time going back ashore; they jumped into the water and swam across. Each of the five destroyers in the force was packed with 800 men. Lines were cast off; the destroyers backed away and steamed into deeper water, where 500 men from each were transferred to the cruisers. The operation took more than an hour longer than planned, and it was 3:20 a.m. before the task force could head for home.

At that point the *Imperial's* rudder, damaged by the near miss on the run up, gave way and she slewed off course, nearly hitting the destroyer *Kimberley* before drifting to a stop. The *Imperial's* rudder was beyond immediate repair. Rear Admiral Henry Rawlings, the group's commander, reluctantly ordered her sunk. Her men were crowded onto the *Hotspur,* which then sent two torpedoes into the *Imperial.* The destroyer was still settling beneath the surface as the

Hotspur, jammed with 900 soldiers and two ships' crews, ran for Kasos Strait.

Rawlings slowed the rest of his squadron to wait for the *Hotspur.* But the delay cost the British precious time: At dawn, the Germans found the seven-ship force still in Kasos Strait. They swarmed about like maddened hornets, plunging through antiaircraft fire to deliver their bombs. The destroyer *Hereward* was the first ship put out of action. She drifted toward Crete, where some Italian vessels later rescued her crew—and 450 soldiers who had only just escaped the Germans.

The next victim was the destroyer *Decoy;* a near miss reduced her speed to 25 knots, and again Rawlings had to slow the rest of the squadron to protect one of his ships. Another near miss on the flagship *Orion* slowed her, and the rest of the fleet, to 21 knots. Then a plane strafed the *Orion's* bridge, killing her captain and wounding Admiral Rawlings.

The cruiser *Dido* was next; she took a direct hit. Lieut. Commander Hugh Hodgkinson, the *Hotspur's* executive officer, was watching when the German bomb hit the cruiser: "A great sphere of black smoke burst out from ahead of her bridge and a single sticklike object curled up into the air and dropped smoking into the sea," Hodgkinson related. "It was one of her guns from a fore turret. Then she seemed to come steaming out of the blackness like a miracle and she was engaging aircraft with her after guns." But the German bomb had also caused destruction below, wrecking the Marines' mess, which had been packed with rescued soldiers, and killing or wounding 84 men.

The assault had been raging steadily for nearly three hours when a bomb smashed through the bridge of the *Orion,* wrecked the lower conning tower and exploded on the stokers' mess deck, which was crowded with troops from Herakleion's jetty; 260 men were killed, 280 more were wounded. Amid the carnage, fire broke out and the *Orion's* controls were damaged. By the time the wounded were sorted out from the dead and emergency steering arrangements had been organized, the *Orion,* her fuel fouled by sea water, could only hiccup along at speeds that fluctuated wildly between 12 and 25 knots. Finally, after six hours under fire, the British watched in relief as the gull-winged Stukas headed back to Scarpanto. At 1 o'clock, however, the ships were attacked by high-altitude bombers; the attacks were repeated at 1:30 and 3 p.m.

Night had fallen by the time the mangled ships came into Alexandria harbor. Their twisted gun turrets poked in every direction. Smoke seeped through jagged holes in their decks. The *Orion* listed in the water as she was pulled along on a towline. From one of the ships came the wail of a bagpipe, and the harbor searchlights picked out a Highlander standing on the ship's bridge. As the battered vessels eased toward their wharves, the only sound in the night was the defiant music of the Scotsman echoing across the harbor.

Cunningham, waiting at the docks, was shocked at the condition of Rawlings' squadron. "I shall never forget the sight of those ships coming up harbor," he wrote, "their upper decks crowded with troops, and the marks of their ordeal only too plainly visible." For more than an hour thereafter, a line of stretchers filed ashore with the casualties: the rescued and the rescuers, wounded and dead.

When evacuations ended on June 1, fewer than 16,000 of the approximately 50,000 men who had reached Crete from Greece had been taken off the island to fight again. The rescued men made a point of thanking the Navy with gifts. The New Zealanders took up a collection and presented £900 to the Navy's charities. Australian soldiers rewarded the sailors with 29,000 bottles of beer that they had somehow managed to bring out with them.

The action at Crete had been costly to the Germans; they had lost 6,000 men in 10 days of fighting. But the British Mediterranean fleet had suffered grievous losses. Three cruisers and six destroyers had been sunk. Two battleships, the carrier *Formidable,* two cruisers and two destroyers had been damaged so badly that they would have to be sent home for repair. Nearly 2,000 sailors had been lost.

The shifting tide of battle in the Mediterranean had turned again, this time strongly against the British. The earlier British victories over the Italian Navy paled in the face of the resounding defeats dealt by the Luftwaffe. And, as bad as the British situation seemed, it would soon get worse.

AID FOR A FALTERING ALLY

A Junkers-88 bomber, part of a crack Luftwaffe squadron that was sent south to attack Malta, is serviced at a bucolic airfield in Sicily in May of 1941.

A DEADLY INFLUX OF STUKAS AND U-BOATS

"There was no doubt we were watching complete experts," wrote Admiral Sir Andrew Cunningham of the Stuka pilots who attacked the British aircraft carrier *Illustrious* on January 10, 1941. "We could not but admire the skill and precision of it all." He might have paid the same compliment to the U-boat captains of the German 29th Flotilla who followed the Luftwaffe into the Mediterranean later the same year, sinking the carrier *Ark Royal* and blowing the battleship *Barham* out of the water within weeks of their arrival. They were all experts, these confident young airmen and submariners, and they had come to Italy to help the faltering Italian forces protect the Axis convoys ferrying troops and supplies to North Africa.

The German pilots whose destructive skill won grudging British admiration belonged to Fliegerkorps X—the 10th Air Corps. As they arrived from Norway, the pilots quickly dispersed their 300 aircraft—Stukas, Ju-88s, Heinkel-111s and Messerschmitt fighters—among the airfields at Catania, Comiso, Trapani, Palermo and Reggio Calabria. The submariners shared the Italian facilities at La Spezia, and had their own base at Salamis in occupied Greece. Though they missed their beer and dumplings, the Germans of both services were warmed by the Mediterranean sun, wine and admiring women. And they trained constantly to keep their skills razor-sharp. Dive-bombing a destroyer, said a Ju-88 pilot, "is like trying to catch a fish with your hands. It needs practice, patience and very swift reactions."

Late in the year, after Fliegerkorps X had been shifted to cover the eastern Mediterranean, Fliegerkorps II moved to Sicily from the Russian front. They took over the task of subduing Malta with equal skill and determination, and by the following spring the German commander in Italy, Field Marshal Albert Kesselring, reported proudly: "During the period March 20 to April 28, 1942, in 5,807 sorties by bombers, 5,667 by fighters and 345 by reconnaissance aircraft, 6,557,231 kilograms of bombs were dropped." He concluded with only slight exaggeration, "The naval and air bases of Malta were put completely out of action."

Admirals Erich Raeder of Germany (center) and Arturo Riccardi of Italy (left) meet at Merano in the Italian Alps in 1941 to discuss joint operations.

Crewmen of the U-97 stand at parade rest as their submarine enters Messina harbor after a patrol in the eastern Mediterranean in September of 1942.

A U-boat of Germany's 29th Flotilla slices the surface just before sunset in August 1942, when Axis power was running at high tide in the Mediterranean.

THE U-BOATS' BOLD STROKES

Late in 1941, U-boats destroyed three of the proudest British warships operating in the Mediterranean. The battleship *Barham* and the cruiser *Galatea* were sunk near Alexandria by the *U-331* and the *U-557* respectively. And, almost in the shadow of Gibraltar, Lieut. Commander Friedrich Guggenberger's daring claimed one of the greatest prizes ever to fall to a U-boat.

Speeding boldly on the surface with an eastward tide, Guggenberger took his *U-81* past the Rock into the Mediterranean on the night of November 12, dodging destroyers and trawlers in the darkness while the beam from a Spanish lighthouse lit up his submarine. The next afternoon he found his prey: an array of carriers, destroyers and a battleship heading home to Gibraltar from Malta. A quick look, a single spread of torpedoes, and Guggenberger had struck the mighty carrier *Ark Royal*. She sank the next day.

Only a skeleton crew remains on the sinking Ark Royal, holed by a German torpedo near Gibraltar.

The 31,100-ton Barham explodes within five minutes of being hit by three torpedoes from the U-331 that rocked the battleship nearly onto her beam-ends.

109

Ordnance men in Sicily prepare to tow sleds loaded with 500-pound bombs to a row of Malta-bound Luftwaffe bombers.

A Ju-88 roars over the harbor at Valletta in April 1942 at the height of the Axis effort to knock out Malta from the air.

German bombs straddle the freighter Dorset on August 13, 1942, as she steams toward Malta. A final attack sank the ship before she reached the island.

BOMBARDING MALTA AT HIGH COST

"Their flak was certainly not to be trifled with," said Luftwaffe Captain Helmut Mahlke after returning from Malta with an enormous shell hole in the wing of his Stuka bomber. Indeed, the pilots and crews of Fliegerkorps X and II needed every iota of skill they could muster—as well as a large measure of luck—to survive their missions. Once over the bristling British outpost they encountered a lethal curtain of antiaircraft fire—"a black wall streaked with flashes," as another German described it.

Withering ground fire was not the only hazard the German airmen confronted. Malta's contingent of Hurricanes and Spitfires lay in wait to pick off the German planes when they broke formation to begin their bombing dives.

Together, the flak and the fighter planes constituted a deadly defensive combination: The air battle for Malta cost the Axis 1,126 aircraft.

Bearded submariners of the U-97 strike a jaunty pose in the conning tower of their vessel, berthed at La Spezia harbor in April of 1942. The sea horse painted on the side was the unofficial insignia of the U-97.

Three weary Luftwaffe pilots return to their base from a mission over Malta in March 1942. Hundreds of their comrades never returned from the mass raids, which were intended to obliterate the island fortress.

HONORS AND ENJOYMENT BETWEEN MISSIONS

When the Germans in Italy returned from their perilous missions, they embraced life with reckless fervor, knowing that the next sortie might be their last.

"We celebrated all the parties as they came," wrote Herbert Werner, a 23-year-old submarine officer. "They came in rapid succession and were welcomed with desperate abandon." The young Luftwaffe pilots too indulged in whatever diversions came their way in the hours between their flak-filled missions over Malta.

In a grinding campaign, these sailors and aviators had earned their shoreside pleasures. The government showed its appreciation by showering them with decorations. And frequently there were more personal satisfactions—such as the companionship of local women.

"I danced through the night with the young girls," wrote Werner, "and forgot that the oceans were reverberating from a thousand depth charges."

A Luftwaffe bombing group in Sicily celebrates its 5,000th sortie, flown over Malta on April 8, 1942.

Submarine Lieutenant Heinrich Schonder, a brand-new Knight's Cross hanging

from his neck, gets a congratulatory kiss at dockside. Schonder, captain of the U-77, received the award after reporting that he had sunk three destroyers.

A SPECIAL KIND OF NAVY

A pilotless Italian Navy motorboat, its rudder locked on course, speeds toward its target at 26 knots during a drill. The boat carried 660 pounds of explosives.

ITALY'S ELITE CORPS OF STEALTHY "SEA DEVILS"

The Duke of Spoleto (left), a motorboat enthusiast who helped to establish the Italian Navy's assault units, confers with three of his officers.

"Everyone has the jitters, seeing objects swimming about at night and hearing movements on ships' bottoms. It must stop." The speaker was no less than Admiral Sir Andrew Cunningham, Commander in Chief of Britain's Mediterranean fleet, describing the mood of his men following a raid by six Italian Navy frogmen, who in December of 1941 had slipped into Alexandria harbor and crippled two Royal Navy battleships and a destroyer.

The attack on Alexandria was the most notable success of a little-heralded but devastatingly effective arm of Italy's Navy: the special assault units. Ultimately these units would sink or disable 86,000 tons of Allied warships and 131,527 tons of merchant shipping.

Working their havoc with speedy motorboats, miniature submarines and torpedo-like submersibles that rode on or as much as 100 feet below the surface, the self-styled "Sea Devils" penetrated harbor defenses and struck before the enemy knew what had hit them. The special assault teams first triumphed in March 1941, when six pilots steered explosive-laden motorboats through a gantlet of mines and antipersonnel nets into Crete's Suda Bay. Each man chose his target from the British ships moored in the bay, and attacked. "I jammed the rudder, released the safety catch and dropped into the water," recalled Sublieutenant Angelo Cabrini. "A few seconds later, I heard a violent explosion. Immediately afterward, I saw the cruiser take a heavy list."

Cabrini, who was pulled out of the water by a British patrol boat, had scored a direct hit on the H.M.S. *York (pages 128-129);* three other pilots were also successful that day, sinking two tankers and a steamer. Heartened by their coup at Suda Bay, the Italians six months later slipped three two-man torpedoes into Gibraltar harbor, where they crippled two freighters and a Royal Navy tanker.

The raids on Suda Bay, Gibraltar and subsequently Alexandria put the British fully—and nervously—on guard against surprise attack. But that did not stop the special assault units; before the battle for control of the Mediterranean was over, they would sink nearly a score more ships

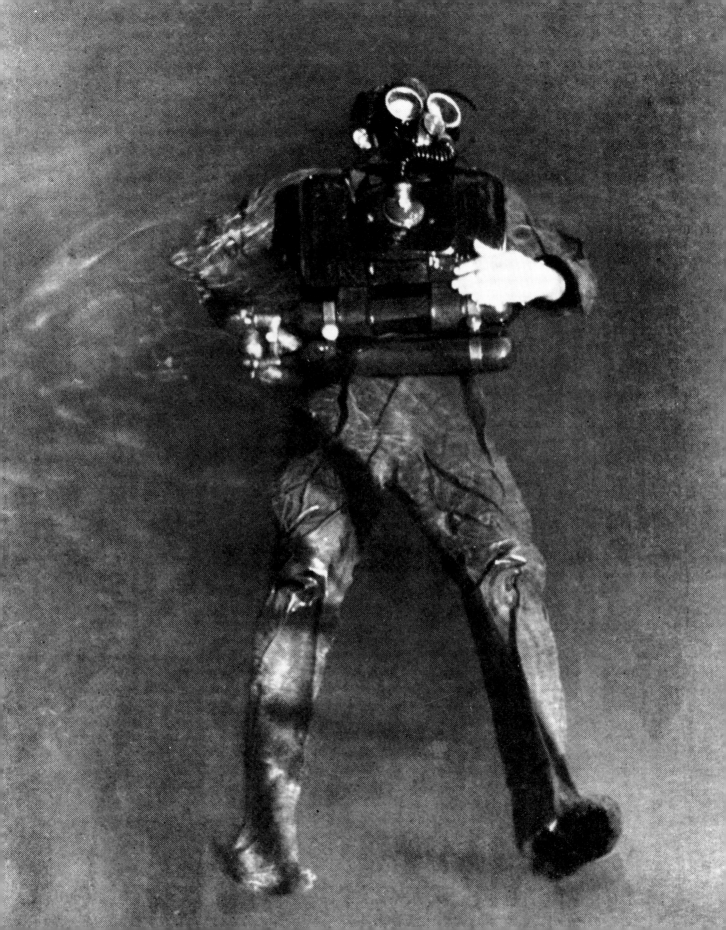

A pilot in training (top) aims his E-boat at a test target. When the pilot was sure of his aim, he accelerated to top speed, locked the rudder in place and jumped overboard. Once in the water (bottom) he floated on the boat's backrest, designed to serve as a life raft.

Under their commander's watchful eye, sailors of the surface division of the 10th Light Flotilla complete maintenance work on a torpedo. Based at the ports of La Spezia and Livorno in northern and central Italy, the flotilla ranged as far east as the Black Sea.

The crew of a two-man assault boat docks after a mission. This boat carried depth charges and torpedoes, and had twin 2,500-horsepower engines that generated a top speed of 30 knots.

AN ODDBALL ARMADA OF HIGH-SPEED ATTACKERS

Many a convoy seaman on night watch was startled to see his ship come under attack by a pack of small, whippet-fast craft known to the British as E-boats. The E stood for explosive, and the term was applied broadly to several different types of motorboats that the Italians used with aggressive abandon against vessels much larger than their own.

The most spectacular of the explosive motorboats were those designed for one-way missions (opposite, top). The flimsy 19-foot craft, whose propeller and rudder could be lifted out of the water to clear harbor nets, was aimed at a target vessel by the lone pilot, who then abandoned ship and swam for his life. If his aim was true, the impact of his boat on the target triggered a chain reaction: A ring of explosives split the E-boat's hull fore and aft.

explosives, sank to a preset depth (determined by the draft of the most likely targets), at which time a water-pressure fuse detonated the charge. The result: a gaping hole torn in the hull of the enemy ship below the waterline.

The Italian special assault units also utilized more conventional boats to great effect—two-man assault boats (above) and larger boats (overleaf) that were equipped with a variety of offensive weaponry. In a typical attack, several such craft would race toward a convoy from both sides, fire their torpedoes, then retreat at full speed. This maneuver would be repeated until the E-boats either had expended their torpedoes or were driven off. The tactic frequently proved devastating: Striking at one convoy bound for Malta in August 1942, an E-boat pack sank a cruiser and four

Ignoring an audience of children, two Italian sailors work on an E-boat between missions. This 48-foot version carried two 17.7-inch torpedoes and two 6.5mm machine guns, and traveled at speeds up to 42 knots.

Two motorboats plow through the wake of a third as their patrol heads out to sea in search of enemy ships. Scores of civilian small craft were converted for use by the Navy after Italy entered the War in June of 1940.

Steel tubes fastened to the deck of an Italian submarine stand open to receive a pair of 22-foot two-man torpedoes. The watertight tubes also could be used to transport a scaled-down model of the one-man E-boat.

"EVERYTHING IS COLD, DARK AND SILENT"

"Hello! Jack Tar, what a beautiful day! / We frogmen are coming to teach you to swim, / So we hope you're all right and we hope that you're trim. / We dive but you go down to stay." So sang the crews of the Italian Navy's two-man torpedoes and miniature submarines. And from the time Italy entered the War, they backed up their taunting ditty with brave deeds.

At the torpedo's top speed of only 2.5 knots, the frogmen rode through harbor defenses with only their heads above water. Even at night, under blackout conditions, they could easily single out a ship

of a match," explained one pilot, "or a snatch of singing may remind you that what you are seeking to destroy is alive.

"You take a compass bearing, then you flood the diving tank; the water closes over your head. Everything is cold, dark and silent."

Once in position under the enemy ship, the frogmen would gingerly detach the 660-pound explosive from their torpedo's nose, secure it to the ship's keel, and set the timer. Then, still mounted on the torpedo, "you start the motor, glide away from the ship, and surface. Finally you can

In this series of underwater photographs, a frogman re-enacting a mission approaches the submarine's deck tube (upper left) and extracts the motorized torpedo (upper right). At bottom left he tests the controls before he and his crewman get under way (bottom right)

The two crewmen of a CB-class midget submarine enjoy some fresh air while they wait for the boat's batteries to recharge. One mission that was never carried out called for an even smaller submersible to be transported across the Atlantic by a mother submarine and released to attack New York Harbor

DURHAM, 10,900 TONS, GIBRALTAR, SEPTEMBER 1941

QUEEN ELIZABETH, 32,000 TONS, ALEXANDRIA, DECEMBER 1941

BARON DOUGLAS, 3,900 TONS, GIBRALTAR, JULY 1942

RAVEN'S POINT, 1,900 TONS, GIBRALTAR, JULY 1942

HARMATTAN, 4,600 TONS, ALGIERS, DECEMBER 1942

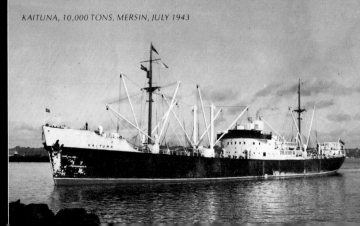
KAITUNA, 10,000 TONS, MERSIN, JULY 1943

VICTIMS OF THE 10TH LIGHT FLOTILLA

The deadliest of the Italian Navy's special units was the 10th Light Flotilla, whose crack assault teams wrought devastation in Allied harbors and seaways all across the Mediterranean. The flotilla's total score was 28 ships sunk or damaged. That figure included the battleships *Queen Elizabeth* and *Valiant* and the cruiser *York,* as well as 111,527 tons of merchant shipping. A partial gallery of the 10th Light Flotilla's victims is presented here, with the tonnage of each ship and the place and month in which it went down.

The feats of the Italian assault teams aroused consternation among the British, and some unabashed envy as well. When the Admiralty set up a school to create its own naval assault units, the trainees pinned magazine photographs of the 10th Light Flotilla on their walls.

VALIANT, 31,000 TONS, ALEXANDRIA, DECEMBER 1941

JERVIS, 1,700 TONS, ALEXANDRIA, DECEMBER 1941

META, 1,600 TONS, GIBRALTAR, JULY 1942

EMPIRE CENTAUR, 7,000 TONS, ALGIERS, DECEMBER 1942

MAHSUD, 7,500 TONS, GIBRALTAR, MAY 1943

CAMERATA, 4,900 TONS, GIBRALTAR, MAY 1943

FERNPLANT, 7,000 TONS, ISKENDERUN, AUGUST 1943

STANRIDGE, 6,000 TONS, GIBRALTAR, AUGUST 1943

The 10,000-ton British cruiser York lies half-submerged at Suda Bay in Crete following an attack by a pack of Italian explosive boats in March of 1941. The Italians were outraged by a German claim that Luftwaffe raids had been responsible for crippling the warship.

4

The German conquest of Greece in April of 1941 led to a poignant exchange of cables between Washington and London. President Roosevelt betrayed his fears that the entire Mediterranean theater might be lost. "In the last analysis," he added, in an attempt to console Churchill, "the naval control of the Indian Ocean and the Atlantic Ocean will in time win the War."

When Churchill received this message he had just returned from Plymouth, which the Luftwaffe had severely bombed. United States Ambassador John Winant found the Prime Minister "tired and depressed"—and angry at Roosevelt's assumption that Britain might be forced to give up the Mediterranean. Once before, when his aides had reported that British commanders in the Middle East were preparing contingency plans for relinquishing Egypt, Churchill had growled that the Joint Chiefs had better set up some firing squads "to shoot the generals." Now it required the combined persuasion of Ambassador Winant, Foreign Secretary Anthony Eden and Deputy Prime Minister Clement Attlee to talk Churchill out of sending an indignant reply to Washington.

Churchill finally settled for a mild rejoinder: "We must not be too sure that the consequences of the loss of Egypt and the Middle East would not be grave." He also seized the occasion to make a bold appeal: "Mr. President, I am sure that you will not misunderstand me if I speak to you exactly what is in my mind. The one decisive counterweight I can see would be if the United States were immediately to range herself with us as a belligerent power. If this were possible I have little doubt that we could hold the situation in the Mediterranean until the weight of your munitions gained the day." But that was six months before the attack on Pearl Harbor, and Churchill must have known that not even President Roosevelt could persuade the Americans to declare war.

Roosevelt's reply was apologetic but evasive. "I did not intend to minimize in any degree the gravity of the situation, particularly as regards the Mediterranean. I am well aware of its strategic importance and I share your anxiety in regard to it." He promised that within three weeks at least 30 merchant ships would leave the United States with supplies for Britain's Middle East forces. Roosevelt made no comment on Churchill's appeal for a U.S. declaration of war.

"SHOCK AFTER SHOCK"

For Britain, the only bright spot on the horizon that month was the dramatic bulletin that reached Whitehall at 4 a.m. on June 22. Churchill's secretary, Jack Colville, had instructions not to wake the Prime Minister for anything short of the invasion of England, so he waited until 8 a.m. before knocking on his door. Churchill's first reaction to the news was to send his valet to awaken Eden (who was staying the night after a late meeting) with a silver salver bearing a large cigar and the note: "The Prime Minister's compliments and the German armies have invaded Russia."

Buoyed by the prospect of some relief in the pressures on the Mediterranean, Churchill addressed the nation, welcoming the Soviet Union as a cobelligerent in the struggle against the Nazis. But within weeks German armies had slashed deep into the Soviet Union, and gloom once again descended on Whitehall.

The reverses continued. In addition to enduring new Dunkirks in Greece and later in Crete, the British had been set back in the desert by General Rommel and the Afrika Korps. The brilliant German tank commander had launched his major attack in March, and the Axis armies once more were advancing toward Egypt. In Cyrenaica, only the port city of Tobruk remained in British hands, and it was under constant siege.

General Wavell, in Churchill's view, was unnecessarily hesitant in launching a counterattack against Rommel. General Sir Alan Brooke, Commander in Chief, Home Forces, was kept busy intercepting angry messages from the Prime Minister to Wavell urging him to get moving. In June, when Wavell finally launched his long-planned offensive, it promptly bogged down.

Finally, on the 20th of June, Churchill removed General Wavell from the Middle East command and replaced him with General Auchinleck, whom he first summoned home from his post in India to explain in person the necessity of driving Rommel back across the desert. Then, through July, August and September, the Prime Minister fussed and fumed while Auchinleck insisted on delaying his own counterattack until he had built up sufficient strength. "Pray explain," Churchill would ask General Brooke in tones dripping with sarcasm, "how it is that in the Middle East 750,000 men always turn up for their pay and rations, but when it comes to fighting only 100,000 turn up?" Constant worry had blackened Churchill's mood. Brooke continually had to restrain him from flying to the front himself to demand more positive action.

As bleak as prospects were for the British, they still possessed Malta, the hinge on which the war in the Mediterranean swung. The island's strategic position athwart Rommel's lines of supply had become more important than ever. During the summer and autumn of 1941, Malta benefited from Hitler's preoccupations elsewhere—not least the campaign against the Soviet Union. The Führer had been forced to dispatch most of Fliegerkorps X to North Africa in support of Rommel, and other planes were sent to the Eastern Front. As a result, the air attacks on the little island lessened appreciably.

The Royal Navy, meanwhile, concerned that Malta might become another Crete, had managed to slip some convoys through from Gibraltar with much-needed supplies, troops and planes. Admiral Cunningham had sent every available submarine to Malta, aiming to use the island as a base for attacking Axis convoys to North Africa. Malta's respite from saturation air attacks also provided the opportunity for more warships to join in the convoy-hunting campaign. Churchill responded to the lull by sending half a dozen destroyers and light cruisers from England.

The new attack group became popularly known as the Malta Striking Forces. Its strategy was to employ a combination of reconnaissance by the newly arrived aircraft and a hunter-killer campaign by warships and planes against nearly every convoy that sailed for Rommel's supply ports.

As early as April of 1941 a small task force from Malta had provided a foretaste of what could be accomplished. An Axis convoy bearing German troops and supplies was spotted off the Tunisian coast by planes from Malta, and four destroyers were dispatched from the island to intercept it. After a race southwestward at 26 knots, the task force's commander, Captain Philip Mack, nosed his ships in close to the Kerkenah Banks along the Tunisian coast near the port of Sfax. At 1:58 a.m. on April 16, Mack spotted five transports and three escorting destroyers only six miles away. Slipping swiftly around the convoy until he had the ships silhouetted against the moon, Mack went in for the kill. In two hours of shellfire and torpedo attack he sank four

WANKLYN OF THE "UPHOLDER": BRITAIN'S UNDERSEA ACE

The nemesis of Axis convoys trying to reach North Africa was the Malta-based British 10th Flotilla, composed of stubby U-class submarines with names like the *Urge* and the *Unbeaten*. Deadliest of these was the *Upholder*; in 16 months of operations the crew stitched 21 white stripes to the *Upholder's* black flag, representing her victims: 10 cargo ships, three troop transports, two tankers, two destroyers, an armed trawler—and three submarines.

The men of the *Upholder* were mostly tough veterans with oak-fiber nerves. To a man they worshipped their gentle-voiced, fierce-eyed commander, a tall Scot named Malcolm D. Wanklyn. Indeed, "Wanklyn of the *Upholder*" became known throughout the Mediterranean fleet as the ultimate submariner.

Commander Wanklyn's uncanny abilities as a navigator enabled him to intercept enemy convoys with an almost occult ease. He appeared to possess a special sort of night vision, discerning targets that were invisible to everyone else. Wanklyn was fearless and deft at slipping between escorting warships to strike at the juiciest prizes. And once he had focused on a moving silhouette, he seldom missed. If the first hit failed to sink a ship, he returned relentlessly to finish it off—after waiting out the depth-charge attacks of the frustrated escorts.

On one of Wanklyn's most successful patrols, in May 1941, the *Upholder* sank a 4,000-ton tanker, but suffered irreparable damage to her asdic set and hydrophones when the convoy's destroyers counterattacked. Wanklyn was now unable to track his foes—a predicament that would have prompted most submarine commanders to run for home. Not Wanklyn. He continued the patrol, and three days later slipped around another escort screen to sink a second tanker. By this time the *Upholder's* fuel tanks were running low, her batteries were nearly exhausted, and only two torpedoes remained.

But Wanklyn had made out three big troop transports in the waning evening light. He moved swiftly through a screen of five destroyers and sent the last two torpedoes point-blank into the side of one of the transports, the 17,800-ton *Conte Rosso*. Then he dived beneath the bow of a charging destroyer. Thirty-seven depth charges and a round of tea later, the *Upholder* surfaced and at last set course for Malta. The mission earned Wanklyn the Victoria Cross.

Bearded Lieut. Commander Malcom Wanklyn (center) and some of the submarine Upholder's 32-man crew relax near their base at Lazaretto Creek, Malta.

of the enemy ships. The other four, crippled and listing, drifted onto a sand bar. Two of them sank the next day; the third, a destroyer, was later salvaged by the Italians. Only one ship, a merchantman, survived.

The Axis' only effective defense had been offered by the destroyer *Tarigo,* which tried to take on the entire British attack force. A British shell wrecked the *Tarigo's* bridge and tore off the leg of the captain, Commander Pietro de Cristoforo, but he refused to leave his post. Crudely bandaged, Cristoforo exchanged salvos with the British until he died from loss of blood. The *Tarigo* fought on without him, although she was nearly blown out of the water by the combined British fire. Despite the damage, an ensign managed to fire two torpedoes into the destroyer *Mohawk,* sending her to the bottom. Finally, her steering gear shot away and her deckhouses in flames, the *Tarigo* settled in the water and went under.

Some 1,700 troops and more than 34,000 tons of military matériel sorely needed by Rommel were lost. The sole surviving merchant ship was herself finished off 10 days later in an exercise reminiscent of early-19th Century naval warfare. Lieut. Commander Malcolm D. Wanklyn, captain of the submarine *Upholder (left),* came upon the German transport still aground on the Tunisian beach, her deck jammed with trucks, scout cars and motorcycles. Commander Wanklyn was unable to reach the ship with his torpedoes because she was behind a sand bar, so that evening he sent in a boarding party. Finding the ship deserted, the team planted demolition charges, opened her sea cocks and raced back to the *Upholder* as the transport and her cargo exploded and burned.

The missions of the Malta Striking Forces had been interrupted when every available vessel in Cunningham's command was pressed into service during the desperate evacuations of Greece and Crete. But by early autumn a flotilla of destroyers and cruisers, designated Force K, had arrived at Malta, and it prepared to resume the attacks on convoys to Rommel. At first the results were disappointing: The wary convoy commanders, some of them running eastward all the way to Greece under cover of German planes, managed to elude the Malta-based hunters and slip through to their North African ports. But on November 8 a plump new target took shape: British reconnaissance planes reported a large convoy of Italian and German transports forming at the tip of Italy's boot.

In the Axis convoy were at least five merchantmen and two tankers, escorted by a force of seven Italian destroyers. As the planes from Malta shadowed them, the transports and destroyers moved eastward and were joined by more destroyers and two cruisers. The cruisers took up stations on the flanks of the convoy. Over the ships flew protective fighter planes.

The Malta squadron scrambled into action so fast that some crewmen were left behind. The captain of one cruiser raced after his ship in a launch and got on board just as the antisubmarine boom at the harbor entrance swung closed behind him. Following a path through the island's minefields, two cruisers and two destroyers set off in bright moonlight at 22 knots. They caught up with the convoy 40 minutes after midnight. Maneuvering to place their targets "down moon," the British attackers congratulated themselves that the convoy ahead betrayed no sign of being spotted. Apparently the British had been seen, but the Italian lookouts mistook them for part of the escort.

It was a fatal mistake. Only 18 minutes after sighting the convoy, the British, in pitch-darkness, opened fire on the Italian destroyers with cool precision. The escort captains were so surprised that they could not organize a defense, and the Italian heavy cruisers had no time to turn back and come to the convoy's protection. In less than an hour all the Italian destroyers had been set afire or driven off, and the British warships cut through the transports like wolves through a flock of sheep.

The transport captains made no move to scatter, but plodded straight ahead as if resigned to the slaughter. Some of the ships were torpedoed, others set ablaze by shellfire. Occasionally an Italian destroyer nosed close enough to take a pot shot at the attackers, only to retreat when the heavier British guns fired back. By 1:32 a.m. every transport and tanker was on fire, and by 2:05 the attackers were racing for home. In the British wake the remaining Italian destroyers returned to poke amid the wreckage and rescue the swimming men. Once more the submarine *Upholder* moved in, torpedoing one of the destroyers and sending it to join the rest of the convoy at the bottom of the Mediterranean.

Consternation reigned in Rome. Two of the Italian Navy commanders involved in the convoy operation were fired. From Africa, Rommel complained that his supply lines had been almost completely severed. Axis convoy losses, which had been 28 per cent in September, reached 63 per cent in November. Only 8,400 tons got through that month, the smallest monthly shipping total thus far in the War. And the losses came at the worst time imaginable for the Afrika Korps: On November 18, General Auchinleck finally launched his major attack. More Malta strikes cut away at Rommel's life lines, and the Afrika Korps, starved for men and equipment, retreated westward.

Rommel's cries for help were heard in Berlin. But Hitler was concentrating on his blitzkrieg into the Soviet Union. He could not counter with dive bombers again in the Mediterranean because none could be spared from the Russian front. The only immediate answer was U-boats; Hitler ordered 10 of them detached from duty in the Atlantic and rushed to the Mediterranean. With their arrival, the British momentum provided by the Malta Striking Forces was at once reversed.

On November 13 the *Ark Royal,* the only British aircraft carrier in the Mediterranean at the time (the *Formidable* had steamed to the United States for repairs), was returning to Gibraltar after launching more fighter planes for Malta's airfields. A German submarine penetrated the carrier's destroyer defense and sent a torpedo into her starboard side under the bridge. Severely damaged, the *Ark Royal* managed to keep going. With her crew frantically battling the flames and manning her pumps, she almost made it home: The carrier sank only 25 miles from Gibraltar.

Another major loss occurred 12 days later. Admiral Cunningham was on board the battleship *Queen Elizabeth* patrolling in the central Mediterranean with a task force from Alexandria when, just as he sat down to tea at 4:30 p.m., he heard a thumping noise like cannon fire in the middle distance. Climbing the ladder to the bridge, he saw the accompanying battleship *Barham* listing to port. The *Barham* had been struck by three torpedoes from another German submarine. "The poor ship rolled nearly over onto her beam-ends," Cunningham wrote later of the episode, "and we saw the men massing on her upturned side. A minute or two later there came the dull rumble of a terrific explosion as one of her main magazines blew up. The ship became completely hidden in a great cloud of yellowish-black smoke, which went wreathing and eddying high into the sky. When it cleared away, the *Barham* had disappeared. There was nothing but a bubbling, oily patch on the calm surface of the sea, dotted with the wreckage and the heads of swimmers. It was ghastly to look at, a horrible and awe-inspiring spectacle."

The *Barham* took 56 officers and 806 enlisted men down with her. The U-boat surfaced and escaped, passing so close to the battleship *Valiant* that her men could not lower their guns enough to fire on her, and so fast that the *Valiant* could not turn in time to ram her. Most of the 450 men who survived—among them Vice Admiral Pridham-Wippell—were immobilized for weeks by lacerations from the *Barham's* thick coat of barnacles, which slashed them like a giant cheese grater as they slid down the hull into the water.

The Alexandria fleet returned home, only to be crippled even further the following month—not by U-boats or by Fliegerkorps X but by a daring commando force of only six Italians who did as much damage as was inflicted in any naval battle of the Mediterranean war—and this inside the protected heart of Alexandria harbor.

The commando attack culminated six years of planning and rehearsal. In October of 1935, two Italian sublieutenants proposed an ingenious naval weapon, a form of manned

Three British Albacore bombers—each with a torpedo between its wheels—fly over Malta's rugged shoreline and terraced fields on their way to search for Axis shipping.

Wearing an oversized homemade decoration presented by his crew, U-boat captain Hans-Friedrich von Tiesenhausen (right) accepts the congratulations of his flotilla commander after sinking the British battleship Barham on November 25, 1941. Tiesenhausen soon was awarded a real Knight's Cross for his feat.

torpedo. The Italian Navy seized upon the idea so promptly that the weapon's first test was conducted in La Spezia harbor only three months later. A development team was mustered and the human torpedo, as it became known, was on its way into the Italian arsenal.

As it was refined over the following years, the weapon was a cigar-shaped craft 20 feet long and less than three feet wide. At its forward end was the pilot's seat and a control console with an instrument panel of luminous dials that could be read underwater as well as in darkness. The craft, driven by a battery-powered engine, had a top speed of slightly more than two knots and a range of 20 miles. Three air tanks with pumps could be regulated to submerge the machine or raise it to the surface. A second man rode in a rear seat. He was needed to help with the torpedo's mission: to detach an underwater bomb from the craft and place it beneath an enemy vessel.

This method of warfare dated from the American Revolution, during which the colonials attempted to attach explosive charges to the hulls of British warships. The Italian Navy had used a crude device of the same sort during World War I, and Allied frogmen employed underwater warheads during World War II. But the Italian 10th Light Flotilla, formed in 1940, would perfect the tactic, and with devastating effect.

In countless practice sessions the two-man crews learned how to sneak up on their target with only their heads above the surface, and then submerge. Oxygen-filled respirators provided for breathing and skintight rubber suits helped protect the men from the cold water. Feeling their way along the hull of the target vessel, they attached a clamp to one bilge keel, a finlike underwater projection on the vessel's hull. Passing under the hull, they rose on the other side to attach a second clamp to the other bilge keel. Connecting these clamps was a line from which the bomb and its warhead were suspended. The frogmen tightened the line in order to position the bomb directly under the keel, a warship's most unprotected and most vulnerable spot. They then set the bomb's timer, usually giving themselves an hour or two to escape.

The early attempts to put this new weapon to work were not promising. The first target was Alexandria harbor. The submarine *Iride* was dispatched to Bomba Bay, west of To-

bruk, to rendezvous with a vessel carrying the torpedoes and their pilots. While surfaced in Bomba Bay, the *Iride* was surprised by three low-flying Swordfish biplanes from the British aircraft carrier *Eagle*. Instead of blowing up the *Eagle*, one of her designated targets in Alexandria harbor, the *Iride* was sent to the bottom of Bomba Bay by torpedoes dropped from the *Eagle's* Swordfish.

The 10th Light Flotilla's next operations were simultaneous forays into Alexandria and Gibraltar harbors; they miscarried badly, evidently because of poor reconnaissance. Creeping into Gibraltar on a September night in 1940 with her torpedo craft aboard, the submarine *Scirè* was belatedly notified by radio that there were no British vessels in the harbor worth destroying, so she withdrew. Her sister submarine, the *Gondar*, was likewise informed at the last moment that Alexandria harbor was devoid of significant targets. Then, en route to her home base at La Spezia, the *Gondar* was sighted by a British warship, depth-charged and sunk. Her officers and crew were picked up by the British. Among those rescued was Lieut. Commander Elios Toschi, one of the two inventors of the secret weapon. Neither he nor anyone else from the submarine mentioned anything about their radical mission, and none of their captors inquired.

The Italians persevered and finally succeeded six months later at Gibraltar. Operating from the *Scirè* off Algeciras, Spain, the torpedomen penetrated the harbor defenses, attached their lethal charges to the underside of the British Naval tanker *Denby Dale* and two merchant vessels, and sank all three. The pilots and their divers slipped over to the Spanish shore undetected and escaped. The underwater commandos now were prepared to launch their most daring attack.

One of the participants in the unsuccessful September foray against Gibraltar had been Commander Luigi Durand de la Penne. Now he was given command of an assault on Alexandria harbor scheduled for the final weeks of 1941. On December 12, de la Penne and nine other torpedo crewmen boarded a plane in Rome and flew to the Dodecanese island of Leros. Nine days earlier the *Scirè* had sailed from La Spezia at dusk, the details of her mission unknown to her crew. Off the Italian coast the *Scirè* had been met by a light-

THE TROJAN HORSE THAT HARASSED GIBRALTAR

Conchita Ramognino, Spanish wife of an Italian officer, stands outside her villa, a secret base for Italian frogmen. Birds caged in a peaked window hid a lookout who spied on the harbor.

The Olterra lies in neutral Spanish waters opposite the Rock. In the contemporary Italian diagram (inset), a torpedo crew leaves the hold of the ship as another waits its turn.

For an Axis saboteur, the British warships berthed in Gibraltar harbor and the Allied convoys that periodically swelled its roadstead were an irresistible temptation. They were also damnably difficult to reach: The Rock bristled with guns; searchlights and patrol boats crisscrossed the harbor, and depth charges probed for any suspected intruders. Yet Italian underwater commandos struck fiercely and frequently at Gibraltar's shipping from lairs under the very nose of its defenders.

Early in the War, the raiders operated from a Spanish coastal villa just two miles from Gibraltar, swimming across the bay to attach explosives to Allied ships. But the difficulty these frogmen had in eluding Spanish shore patrols after their missions led the Italians to switch to what a British intelligence officer called a "floating Trojan Horse": The 4,995-ton *Olterra,* a battered Italian merchant ship docked across the bay from Gibraltar.

The Italians replaced most of the *Olterra's* crew with divers and Navy technicians, who built a secret workshop in the ship's hold. It contained everything needed to assemble and repair two-man torpedoes and keep them loaded with explo-

sives. A door was cut six feet below the *Olterra's* waterline so the frogmen and their torpedoes could come and go undetected. The torpedoes were smuggled into Spain disguised as boiler tubes.

The first few attacks from the *Olterra* against warships in Gibraltar's inner harbor proved costly for the raiders: Five of six frogmen sent out did not return, and no damage was done to the ships. But when the Italians turned to merchantmen anchored in the more lightly guarded roadstead, they found easy pickings. All told, the frogmen sank or damaged more than 42,000 tons of Allied shipping, and the British never did discover where they had come from or where they had gone.

er carrying three torpedo craft. After they had been loaded onto special caissons on her deck, the submarine proceeded to Leros and was waiting in the harbor when de la Penne's plane arrived. The *Scirè's* captain, Prince Junio Valerio Borghese, was also a veteran; he had commanded the submarine during both of the missions on Gibraltar.

De la Penne and his fellow frogmen reported aboard the *Scirè*. Two days later, when reconnaissance planes reported fair weather and good hunting in Alexandria harbor, the *Scirè's* camouflage net was furled and she set out for Alexandria. En route to the drop-off point the commandos rested, drinking fruit juices for added vitamins and enjoying the meager comforts of the submarine while they could, knowing that soon they would be diving in the chill waters of the Mediterranean. During the voyage Commander Borghese kept his vessel submerged, partly because of rough seas but primarily to hide from reconnaissance planes.

On the afternoon of December 18, Borghese surfaced off the Egyptian coast to pick up the latest intelligence by radio from Athens. The afternoon air-reconnaissance report was promising: Alexandria harbor was crowded with vessels, including two large battleships. The *Scirè* settled gently to the shallow sea bottom.

In a last-minute council of war, the torpedo crews settled on their targets. De la Penne and his mate, Chief Diver Emilio Bianchi, were to go for the battleship *Valiant*. Lieutenant Antonio Marceglia and Corporal Spartaco Schergat were assigned the battleship *Queen Elizabeth*. The third pair, Lieutenant Vincenzo Martellotta and Chief Diver Mario Marino, were ordered to look for an aircraft carrier. If there were none, they were directed to pass up the tempting cruisers and instead pick out a fuel tanker. Their torpedo craft was armed with extra incendiary explosives to ignite the tanker's oil as it spread across the water, thereby turning the harbor surface into a sheet of fire.

As soon as darkness cloaked the sea above them, the three crews struggled into their black rubber suits ("as oppressive as the strangle hold of a wrestler," de la Penne recalled) and strapped on their respirators and luminous wrist watches. Commander Borghese took the submarine to the surface and the conning-tower hatch was opened. One by one the commandos climbed the narrow steel ladder,

Borghese giving each in turn the traditional kick in the pants for good luck.

The night was silent and calm. Stars sparkled above the men. A mile away they could make out the ghostly spire of Alexandria's blacked-out Ras-el-Tin lighthouse. The frogmen pulled the respirators over their heads. The hatch clanked shut and the submarine quickly settled underwater again, sinking onto the muddy bottom. Standing on the *Scirè's* deck under 35 feet of water, the men struggled to extricate the torpedoes from their caissons.

One of them stuck, and was wrenched loose only after a lengthy tugging match. It was 9 p.m. before all six men were perched on their seats and had started their electric motors humming. They eased to the surface and headed for the darkened shoreline.

Like swimmers in formation, their heads just above the water, the six commandos rode their craft toward the black tower of the lighthouse that marked the entrance to the harbor. When the lighthouse loomed above them, de la Penne checked his watch and found that this leg of the mission had taken two hours, a bit less time than he had expected. The plan was to slip into the harbor at midnight or later, so he called a rest halt. The men had brought along emergency rations in watertight containers, which they now broke open to fortify themselves for the work ahead. As they were eating, a light suddenly flashed over their heads.

It was the lighthouse. Jettisoning their leftovers, the team quickly purred away from the tower, whose beam was stabbing through the darkness. De la Penne guessed what that meant: A warship was returning to the harbor. The entrance boom with its antisubmarine nets would swing open for her. He gave the order to move toward the entrance. As they went slowly along the breakwater, still surfaced, their legs were jarred by short, sharp underwater concussions. The British were depth-charging the area. Had the attackers been sighted? Or was it a routine precaution? In either case it added another hazard to their mission.

Nearing the harbor entrance, the frogmen trimmed their torpedo craft until only the head of each pilot was above water; the divers sitting at the rear had donned their respirators and submerged. Perched on his tilted vehicle, de la Penne could see a small motorboat cutting back and forth in front of the entrance boom, dropping depth charges. Their concussion was painful at this distance, especially for the divers underwater. De la Penne found himself so close to the breakwater that he could hear men talking. As he floated below them in the darkness, signal lights came on at the entrance gate. He motioned to the other two pilots, and all three slid quietly to a buoy near the gate. A light flashed from the buoy, picking out the shape of a blacked-out ship heading for the entrance. The gate would now be opening. De la Penne and his companions submerged and headed for the narrow passage into Alexandria harbor.

De la Penne calculated that he and his diver had just passed the gate entrance when a surge swept them downward. As they touched bottom a huge hull slid above them, its propellers whirring just over their heads. They stayed on the bottom until a second ship had passed over them, then de la Penne gunned his motor to follow the vessel into mid-harbor. Slowing, he cautiously piloted his craft toward the surface. He stuck his head out of the water just as a third ship bore down on them.

The ship's bow wave washed the torpedo craft against another buoy. Neither crew nor craft was hurt nor, evidently, had anyone on board the ship noticed the incident. The other two torpedo craft were nowhere to be seen; if they had made it into the harbor, they would be proceeding to their targets. De la Penne set out for his.

Following the third ship, which he made out to be a destroyer, de la Penne swerved away under her stern when she rounded up to anchor. He studied what he could make out of the harbor. Ahead of him he distinguished two cruisers moored stern to the breakwater. He slipped past their bows. The next vessel in line was a battleship.

As he neared her, de la Penne identified the ship as the Lorraine, one of the French fleet interned in Alexandria. Her bulk hid the next vessel, but when de la Penne rounded the Lorraine's bow, he saw the Valiant, his target. "She was enormous," he recalled later, "a 31,000-ton battleship." He paused to contemplate the ship for a moment. "I was thrilled by the thought," he remembered, "that the strength and daring of only two men were to cripple her."

But not without pain and peril. The Lorraine and the Valiant were bathed in light, and the 1,000 yards of water between them was nearly as well illuminated. With only his head above water and with Bianchi and the torpedo craft submerged, de la Penne inched across the open water toward the high sides of the Valiant. He had nearly reached her when he bumped against an obstruction. It was an antitorpedo net surrounding the British battleship.

Poking along the top of the net, he found a gap between two floats where sections of the net were joined. He brought the torpedo craft to the surface, and he and Bianchi dismounted to try to force their way through the gap. In the process the craft made rasping noises, and the two men froze until they were sure they had not been heard. Something sharp punctured de la Penne's rubber suit, and the cold water stabbed at him. Finally they got their craft through. De la Penne checked his watch again: 2 a.m. He and Bianchi remounted, and de la Penne took a bearing on the Valiant's soaring funnel. He slipped the respirator over his head, submerged 20 feet and headed for the underwater spine of the battleship.

In the pitch-blackness of the harbor bottom they rammed into the hull before seeing it. De la Penne's hands were so numb from the cold water that he fumbled at the controls. The torpedo craft dived for the harbor bottom, its pro-

Members of an Italian assault team stand ready to cast off from Sicily on July 25, 1941, for a raid on Malta that proved fatal to its three leaders. Major Teseo Tesei (second from left), co-inventor of the so-called human torpedo, blew himself up with his craft in order to destroy the net guarding the entrance to Malta's harbor. The commanding officer, Captain Vittorio Moccagatta (second from right), and Lieutenant Giovanni Parodi (right) were killed by a strafing British plane.

pellers still churning. It plowed into the mud and stalled.

De la Penne, attached to his craft by a line, swam to the surface to check his bearings. He was about 45 feet forward of the No. 1 funnel. He pulled himself to the bottom on his line and felt for his diver. Bianchi was gone.

He surfaced again. No Bianchi. But there was no sign on board the big battleship that anyone had noticed the noisy activity under her hull. De la Penne went down again. The torpedo craft's electric motor would not start. Groping for its propellers, he found them snarled in a steel cable, perhaps from the antitorpedo net. He was at the bottom of Alexandria harbor, alone, and with an inoperative boat.

De la Penne decided to drag his craft under the ship. As he struggled through the mud of the harbor bottom, sea water leaked into his respirator; he swallowed it to keep it from blocking his oxygen intake. Stumbling through the mud, he was guided by the sound of one of the *Valiant's* pumps plunking rhythmically a few feet away. When the sound was directly overhead, he bumped against the hull.

De la Penne checked the dim glow of his watch again: He had been thrashing around under the battleship for 20 minutes. His strength was nearly gone. With no diver to help him, he could not detach the bomb and rig it to the bilge keels of the ship. He positioned the torpedo and its bomb in the mud directly under the hull and set the timer. The torpedo craft would blow up with its bomb; he would have to escape without it.

The Italian commando climbed for the surface, emerging with a rush, tearing off his respirator and gasping from his exertions. The noise betrayed him. As he started to swim away, a voice called from the deck. He swam faster. There was a burst of machine-gun fire, and bullets splattered in the water around him. Then he spotted a mooring buoy and quickly swam to it. Clinging to the buoy was Bianchi.

The two men had only a few moments in which to report to each other—Bianchi that he had been knocked off the torpedo and had tried to hide behind the buoy rather than flounder about attracting attention, and de la Penne that the warhead was set to go off under the *Valiant's* hull.

The firing had ceased, but de la Penne decided that they would have to surrender. Their job was done; the rest depended on the bomb and its timer. He noticed a mooring chain running from the buoy to the battleship's bow, and

decided to climb aboard the ship. No sooner was he out of the water than the machine gun opened up again. He dropped back into the water, clung to the buoy and waited for the British to pick them up. He checked his watch again. It was 3:30 a.m. The bomb was set for 6:20.

Admiral Cunningham, asleep in his cabin on the *Queen Elizabeth,* awoke at 4 a.m. to a banging on his door. An aide reported that two Italian frogmen had been discovered hanging onto the *Valiant's* mooring buoy. They had been taken aboard the battleship and had identified themselves but refused to say more. So they had been taken ashore to be grilled by an Italian-speaking interrogator. Cunningham at once replied: Take them back aboard the *Valiant* and imprison them deep in the hold. That might make them talk.

De la Penne was still numb and shivering from his underwater ordeal as he and Bianchi were delivered back to the *Valiant.* One of the guards offered them a warming tot of rum. As he sat in the hold of the battleship, de la Penne confronted a temptation: Since he had not been able to attach the bomb to the bottom of the *Valiant,* the ship was not yet doomed. All he had to do was suggest that she be moved from the mooring, thus saving not only the battleship but his life and Bianchi's as well. No, he decided, he would not. He checked his watch again: A little more than an hour to go. He settled back to await his fate. As for Bianchi, he was so exhausted he fell asleep.

Listening to the slow creak of the ship and the gentle breathing of his companion, de la Penne contemplated his imminent demise. "What would happen in this deep hold during the explosion?" he remembered asking himself as the last minutes ticked by. "Would we die by drowning, or be blown to bits?" Half an hour. He consoled himself with the recollection of the ribbon on the hat of one of his guards: H.M.S. *Valiant.* "Whatever happened to me," he recalled, "I could feel proud that I had fulfilled my mission to the letter. I had not failed my country."

Fifteen minutes. Bianchi still slept. Ten minutes. De la Penne called to his guards and asked to see the captain.

He was whisked topside and met by Captain Charles Morgan and an interpreter. The *Valiant,* de la Penne announced, would blow up in a few minutes. The captain should give orders to abandon ship. Morgan asked for more details. De la Penne would say no more. Morgan ordered him returned to the hold. As he was led below, de la Penne could hear the ship's loudspeakers crackling with the order to abandon ship.

The compartment door scarcely had clanged shut when there was a muffled explosion and the battleship shuddered. The lights went out. De la Penne was thrown across the compartment, wrenching his knee. Bianchi was rudely awakened. The ship heeled onto her side. Smoke seeped through the door.

De la Penne tried the door and found it unlocked and unguarded. Feeling their way out through the smoky darkness, he and Bianchi located a steel ladder and climbed it, emerging through a hatch onto the bridge. It was empty.

The two Italians worked their way aft, where some of the *Valiant's* officers were gathered on the canted deck near the stern. Everyone was looking toward the nearby *Queen Elizabeth*. As they—and their two attackers—watched, the other battleship seemed to rise out of the water. There was a thundering explosion; a shower of scrap flew from her funnel; fuel oil sprayed into the air, some of it drenching the *Valiant's* afterdeck. "Then I knew," de la Penne exulted, "that the brave efforts of Marceglia and Schergat had met with entire success!" He did not know, but soon found out, that the third crew had been almost equally successful. Their bomb had torn the stern off the tanker *Sagona* and damaged the destroyer *Jervis* berthed alongside. But the incendiary explosives had failed, and at least Alexandria harbor was spared being turned into a fiery caldron.

Nevertheless, this daring assault by six submarine commandos had done more damage to the Royal Navy in the Mediterranean than had the entire Italian fleet. Britain's last two battleships in the theater would be out of commission for months. Admiral Cunningham was frank in his communiqué to the First Sea Lord, Sir Dudley Pound: "We are having shock after shock out here," he wrote. "The damage to the battleships at this time is a disaster." Remembering the episode later, he added, "One cannot but admire

GALLANT TRIBUTE TO A HUMANE FOE

Italian Commander Luigi Durand de la Penne.

Admiral Sir Charles Morgan of the Royal Navy was mightily impressed by the Italian officer who had blown the battleship *Valiant* out from under him. Commander Luigi Durand de la Penne had led three teams of frogmen into Alexandria harbor on December 19, 1941, to plant explosive charges under the hulls of British warships. De la Penne was captured almost at once, and moments before the charges exploded he warned Morgan, giving him time to evacuate the *Valiant's* lower decks and avoid any loss of life.

Morgan never forgot that humane gesture. Indeed, his admiration for his foe grew when, after Italy had surrendered, de la Penne assisted British frogmen in a raid on a German Naval installation at La Spezia in 1944. Morgan, who by then was commanding Royal Navy forces in the Adriatic, tried to obtain a British medal for de la Penne for his role in that raid. He was thwarted, however, because though Britain and Italy were cooperating, they were not formal Allies.

Then in March of 1945 the admiral got a chance to repay chivalry with chivalry. Morgan was accompanying Crown Prince Umberto of Italy on an inspection tour of the Naval barracks at Taranto. The Prince was to present medals to several Italian sailors—among them de la Penne, who was to be awarded the *Valor Militare*, Italy's highest decoration, for leading the raid on Alexandria.

As Commander de la Penne stepped forward to receive his medal, Prince Umberto—who knew of Morgan's efforts to decorate his former adversary—turned to the admiral and exclaimed, "Come on, Morgan, this is your show."

"I thus had the pleasure and honor," recalled Morgan, "of decorating de la Penne for the very courageous and gallant attack he made on my ship."

Admiral Morgan presents the Italian Valor Militare to de la Penne (second from right) for his raid on Alexandria, which even Churchill praised for its "extraordinary ingenuity."

the cold-blooded bravery and enterprise of these Italians.''

None of them escaped. De la Penne and Bianchi were imprisoned at Alexandria. Martellotta and Marino, who had successfully fixed their bomb to the tanker *Sagona,* scuttled their craft, swam ashore, hid their rubber suits and sauntered through the dockyard. They made it as far as the dockyard gates before a suspicious guard arrested them.

Marceglia and Schergat, who had holed the *Queen Elizabeth,* rode their torpedo boat to a nearby beach, sank it, got out of their rubber suits and slipped past the port patrols and into Alexandria, where that afternoon they took refuge in a bar, posing as French sailors. Next day the two boarded a train to Rosetta, 35 miles northeast of Alexandria; they spent the night in a hotel there before preparing to embark from a nearby beach, where by prearrangement the Italian submarine *Saffiro* was awaiting them.

The next day, December 20, the two men made their way to the beach to meet the *Saffiro's* boat. Instead they found Egyptian police waiting for them. They had been betrayed not by anyone in Egypt but by careless intelligence work in Rome: Their escape kits contained British £5 notes, one of which they had used in the Alexandria bar, little knowing that the British, for diplomatic reasons, used only Egyptian currency in Egypt.

All six frogmen were handed over to the British Army as prisoners of war. Cunningham requested that they be isolated for six months in the hope that the enemy would not realize the extent of the devastation they had caused. Meanwhile Cunningham did what he could to deceive the Axis. The damage to the *Valiant* was too great to hide; she had to go into dry dock or sink. But it was possible to correct the

Queen Elizabeth's list by counterflooding her compartments so that she sat on an even keel at her shallow mooring. Cunningham continued to live on board, and he distributed a photograph of the ship's band and color guard, on board as usual at a hoisting of the colors, as if the battleship were not sitting on the bottom with her hold full of water.

December of 1941 was indeed a time of shock after shock for the Allies. Two weeks before the frogmen's attack on Alexandria, the news had come from the Pacific that the Japanese had entered World War II by destroying a large part of the U.S. fleet at Pearl Harbor in an attack reminiscent of Taranto. Britain now had her long-awaited ally. Prime Minister Churchill was delighted: ''To have the United States at our side was to me the greatest joy,'' he wrote later. ''United we could subdue everybody else in the world.'' But in Alexandria, the long-range benefit of the U.S. entry into the War was offset for the time being by the need to drain even more ships from the Mediterranean to meet the new challenge in the Pacific, particularly when, on December 10, Japanese torpedo planes sank the prized British warships *Repulse* and *Prince of Wales* off the coast of Malaya. During the month of December, no fewer than 13 capital ships of the British and U.S. Navies, nearly half their combined strength, were sunk or put out of commission. And in Berlin in December, Hitler decided finally to put Malta out of the War.

His was a two-part plan. From the Russian front, where winter weather had bogged down the German drive eastward, the Luftwaffe's Fliegerkorps II was transferred to Sicily to launch an all-out effort to destroy Malta, taking up where Fliegerkorps X had left off when it was ordered to North Africa. Simultaneously, plans went ahead for Operation *Hercules,* an invasion of the island, if that became necessary in order to eliminate this last source of harassment of Rommel's supply lines.

On December 21, the stepped-up German air attacks began. By the end of December the number of air raids for the month had risen to 169; this was 76 more than the monthly average achieved by Fliegerkorps X during its saturation bombing a year earlier. January 1942 brought 262 sorties of high-altitude and dive bombers over the little island, more than eight raids per day. Nearly 2,500 Luftwaffe planes blasted Malta in February, and twice that many attacked in

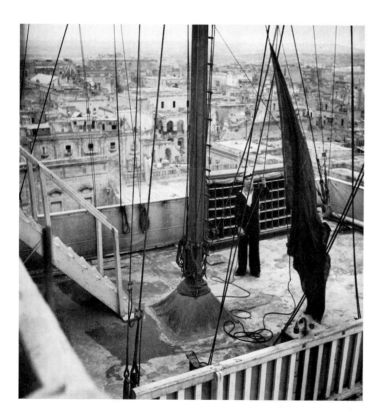

Atop a building in Valletta, Malta's capital, British sailors hoist a red flag to warn of approaching Axis bombers. Malta was hit by twice as many bombs in two months of 1942 as fell on London in the year-long Blitz.

Ack-ack bursts and bomb smoke enshroud Malta's Grand Harbor during an air raid in the spring of 1942. The island's antiaircraft gunners were remarkably accurate, taking a toll of Axis airmen equal to their own losses.

March. The island's Hurricane defenders were virtually swept from the air. By the end of January only 28 were left, feverishly kept in repair by stubborn ground crews using parts cannibalized from the wrecked planes that littered the island. By mid-February, only 11 were capable of flying. Malta lay cut off and helpless under constant bombardment from the air.

In desperation, Cunningham assembled what ships he could in March, and from Alexandria sent off a convoy of food, fuel and ammunition in four fast merchant ships es-corted by cruisers and destroyers. On the third day out they were attacked by the Luftwaffe and by the Italian Navy, whose commanders had been encouraged by the news of the Royal Navy's losses. As it turned out, the Mediterranean itself came to the British Navy's aid, blowing a gale that helped drive off the Italian fleet. But Fliegerkorps II was waiting for the supply ships as they approached Malta. Three of the vessels, badly damaged, made it into the harbor while thousands of Maltese, unmindful of falling bombs, stood on the cliffs and cheered. Then, in the harbor, the

ships were plastered by an intense carpet-bombing attack; all of them sank within sight of the anguished islanders. Of 26,000 tons of cargo sent from Alexandria, only 5,000 tons were salvaged.

Malta's dockyards were crippled. The majority of Cunningham's destroyers and cruisers fled for Alexandria and Gibraltar, and the submarines had to remain submerged during daylight hours to escape the bombs. The island's Victory Kitchens, which had been set up in 1941 to feed the homeless, were now providing 200,000 meals each day. The daily bread ration was reduced to 10 ounces. There was no fuel for light or power.

From the west came further attempts to keep Malta alive. Not since the *Ark Royal* had been sunk in November of 1941 had reinforcements of aircraft been brought from Gibraltar. On March 7, 1942, the aging carriers *Eagle* and *Argus* managed to get close enough to fly in 15 new Spitfires, which proved a better match than the Hurricanes for the Germans' Messerschmitt-109s. Later in March, the carriers sent in 16 more Spitfires. Malta's strengthened air defenses shot down 37 Luftwaffe attackers that month. But the massive bombardment continued. And when, in one of the earliest U.S. actions in the European war, the American carrier *Wasp* transported 47 Spitfires into the Mediterranean, Flie-

gerkorps II was waiting for them. They were pounced upon as soon as they landed at Malta; in an almost continuous three-day raid, nearly all the new planes were destroyed on their airstrips.

Still, on May 9 the *Wasp* and the *Eagle* came back, this time with 64 Spitfires. Profiting from bitter experience, the island's ground crews had perfected a speeded-up system of refueling. The new Spitfires arrived in the midst of an air raid. After landing and racing to their refueling stations, they were back in the air within minutes. For the first time, the Messerschmitts of Fliegerkorps II were driven off. By the end of May the loss figures for the attackers had risen to 40 a month, and those of the British defenders had dropped to 25. Even more encouraging to the British was the May statistic for planes destroyed on the ground: six. In April it had been 30. Fliegerkorps II's onslaught had been blunted for the moment. If the Axis wanted to put Malta out of the War, evidently the only alternative was Operation *Hercules*.

But Malta was saved from invasion, and by—of all people—Rommel. In January 1942 the "Desert Fox," his convoys moving freely while Malta was under attack, had launched a major counterassault. General Auchinleck's army had been driven back again, all the way to a line between Gazala and Bir Hacheim, just west of Tobruk. Here Rommel was ordered to wait until Operation *Hercules* had finally secured his supply lines by capturing Malta. But Rommel, concerned about the possibility of a counterattack, persuaded the German High Command to let him advance again to keep the British on the defensive. New target dates were set: another attack in the desert on May 26, and Operation *Hercules* on July 10.

Rommel's target this time was Tobruk. After an overwhelming assault that included more than 350 tons of bombs from the air, Tobruk's stubborn defenders, who had held out through nine months of siege, at last surrendered on June 21. Exultantly, Hitler promoted Rommel to field marshal. For the Allies the fall of Tobruk was a shattering blow to morale. They did not realize at the time that its loss had saved Malta.

Rommel was so encouraged by the war supplies captured in Tobruk—2,000 trucks and tanks, 1,400 tons of fuel, 5,000 tons of rations—that he urged Hitler to let him keep the pressure on in the desert war. The Führer agreed, and Operation *Hercules* was postponed once more. At the end of June, Rommel drove eastward again, and the British retreated all the way to El Alamein, where both exhausted armies paused to regroup. With Rommel promising to capture Cairo by the first week in July, an elated Mussolini flew to North Africa to be in on the triumph.

In Alexandria, only 60 miles from El Alamein, the British Navy had a new Mediterranean commander in chief. Cunningham had reluctantly accepted orders to head the British delegation to the Anglo-American Combined Chiefs of Staff office in Washington, and had left the Mediterranean on April 3, 1942. His successor was Admiral Sir Henry Harwood, recent victor over the German pocket battleship *Admiral Graf Spee* in the battle of the River Plate. Harwood confronted a chilling prospect: The enemy's army and air force were just over the horizon, and the British fleet in Alexandria still had no battleships. In mid-June Harwood had tried again to supply beleaguered Malta. Only two ships had been able to get through from Gibraltar, and an entire convoy from Alexandria had been driven back.

Harwood had no choice but to retreat even from Alexandria, scattering his ships in such ports as Haifa, Port Said and Beirut, and transferring his headquarters to Ismailia on the Suez Canal. Distress verging on panic spread through the fleet. En route to Haifa, the British submarine-depot ship *Medway* was torpedoed by a U-boat, taking to the bottom vital spare parts and 90 desperately needed torpedoes. It was almost the *coup de grâce* to the Royal Navy in the Mediterranean, after two years of war in which resounding success had turned to disaster. Indeed, it seemed as though Roosevelt's fears of a year earlier—that Britain would be driven from the Mediterranean—were coming true.

The skeleton of a Gladiator fighter plane named Faith is saluted in wartime ceremonies awarding it to the Maltese as a historic relic. At one point in the grim early months of the Mediterranean war, Faith and two other planes, dubbed Hope and Charity, defended the island against an Italian force of 200 aircraft, shooting down at least 30 of them.

THE UNQUENCHABLE MALTESE

Malta's defenders at Grand Harbor cheer an arriving British cargo ship, part of a convoy bringing desperately needed supplies to the besieged island.

COPING WITH A CRISIS OF SUPPLY

In January 1942, when Germany's Luftwaffe seized command of the skies over the Mediterranean, the British island fortress of Malta faced a supreme test of survival. Blockaded and assaulted by Junkers bombers, Malta relied wholly on help from the outside: food for its people, arms and ammunition for its defenders, fuel for its outnumbered RAF fighter planes. The island's life lines steadily unraveled: Of 30 cargo ships sent to Malta in convoys during the first seven months of the year, only 10 broke through the German cordon—and three of those were sunk while being unloaded in the island's harbor.

Though their situation was grim, the Maltese responded with grit and ingenuity, stretching to the limit what little they had. Burly stevedores who were used to eating six pounds of bread a day managed to work on a scant 10-ounce dole. Malta-based submarine crews raised pigs in shoreside pens, while soldiers grew crops on the island's race track and polo grounds. To conserve precious cooking fuel, whole neighborhoods pooled their rations at Victory Kitchens, which produced their single daily meal. Communal cooking ensured—as a Maltese woman said cheerfully—that "everyone should starve equally."

To save Malta from starvation or surrender, the Royal Navy also improvised. Minelayers and submarines were converted to cargo carriers. These vessels were able to slip through the enemy blockade and bring Malta vital supplies.

Throughout their ordeal, the people of Malta maintained high spirits. They showered heartfelt appreciation on those outsiders who risked their lives to keep Malta supplied. Wrote a Naval officer of the moving reception given the surviving ships in his battered convoy: "The Maltese had gathered in their thousands at all possible vantage points. As we drew nearer we saw what appeared to be tiny specks of white moving in front of the people, and heard, a little later, the sound of clapping. Those specks proved to be their hands. Then we heard a murmuring in the distance. Spontaneously and unrehearsed they had broken into the strains of the National Anthem."

Supported by crewmen from the Malta garrison, a salvage diver prepares to raise supplies from a cargo ship that was sunk just off the island.

An RAF spotter searches out and tracks attacking planes from a building on Malta. Sightings were relayed to a fighter-control center and to planes in the air.

149

British soldiers—part of a convoy's load—disembark from a harbor tug to reinforce the Malta garrison, which numbered 30,000 men at the beginning of 1942.

TEAMWORK TO GET PRECIOUS CARGO ASHORE

The imminent arrival of a convoy galvanized nearly everyone on Malta into well-rehearsed action. Soldiers manned the island's coastal guns to drive off the planes and submarines that often hounded the cargo ships. Fighter planes from the Maltese airfield met the approaching vessels to protect them from the Luftwaffe. And many civilians deployed for an assortment of chores under combat conditions.

Immediately the ships tied up at Grand Harbor, the unloading began—under the constant threat of air raids. Malta's 15,000 dockyard workers went to extremes to get the cargo quickly ashore and safely stored. They posted children to shout "Danger!" at the approach of German planes and worked until the last possible moment. The dockworkers' wives lent a hand, passing shells to the antiaircraft gunners who covered the harbor. It was little wonder that in what a German general called "an incredibly short time," the freighters had unloaded and sailed back to sea.

Lighters packed with flour, an item that was in chronically short supply on Malta, await unloading at the Grand Harbor docks.

Soldiers off-load supplies from a truck camouflaged to blend with Malta's buildings. A stone archway provides bombproof storage.

Operators in Malta's underground Coastal Defense Plotting Room stand ready to relay messages to and from artillery batteries.

Wooden obstacles (foreground) discourage enemy glider landings on Malta's fields. German bombs explode in the distance.

An antiaircraft crew prepares to repel an air raid. The gunners sent up what one German called "a barrier of fire to be penetrated only by stout hearts."

The submarine Unrivalled returns to her Malta base after a patrol. The 15 submarines of Malta's 10th Flotilla sank nearly 400,000 tons of enemy shipping—

"MAGIC CARPET" SERVICE BY SUBMARINE

British submarines based in Malta continued to strike at enemy shipping long after Axis bombs had driven all surface ships to safer ports. They paid a high price for staying. Their losses were 50 per cent, leading their commander to note ruefully that life would have been "much pleasanter" if submarine pens had been available.

Even so, in a 16-month period the submarines sank no fewer than 75 enemy ships. And while they were busy destroying Axis supplies, other British submarines were carrying precious cargo to the beleaguered island. The "magic-carpet service to Malta," as these stripped-down cargo submarines were called, concentrated on such basics as fuel, ammunition and medicine. But they also carried special consignments: One submarine was said to have arrived at Grand Harbor with its torpedo tubes stuffed with sausages. And they always made room for that great morale-booster, the mail.

One general described the service of the underwater freighters as "relief in penny packets." But the packets, if small, piled up quickly. In the last half of 1941, supply submarines made 16 runs to Malta, each bringing an average of 160 tons of cargo.

In early 1942, when the Axis played havoc with convoys to Malta, the cargo submarines became even more important and efficient, transporting loads averaging 200 tons. Altogether they slipped some 65,000 tons of goods past the enemy—without a single loss.

including 39 supply ships and six tankers—in 16 months of duty at the island.

During a break in air raids, a Malta submarine recharges her batteries.

Sailors ease a torpedo into a submarine preparing to leave port on patrol.

Crewmen unfold an Albacore's wings in a pen designed to stop shrapnel.

A HANDFUL OF DEFENDERS WHO TOOK THE OFFENSE

Malta's air force made up in gallantry what it lacked in numbers. Its spirit originated with the handful of airmen who piloted the force's initial complement of fighter craft—four Gladiator biplanes. One of the aircraft was damaged beyond repair on the first day of air raids, June 11, 1940. But the other three—nicknamed *Faith, Hope* and *Charity*—did battle so effectively that Italian bomber pilots reported an estimated enemy force of 25 planes.

Hurricanes and eventually Spitfires replaced the old-fashioned biplanes. Along with Wellington bombers and Swordfish and Albacores from the Fleet Air Arm, Malta's air force took the War to Axis convoys, sinking or crippling more than 80 enemy ships in 1942 alone.

But the air units suffered heavy casualties themselves. At one point, in March 1942, the fighter planes based at one of Malta's three airfields had been whittled down to only five. To conserve these fighters for their most important job—protecting convoys—they were grounded when enemy bombers plastered the island. The precious planes were parked in blast pens —protective rings of concrete and sandbags built by soldiers and civilians. There, to the airmen's frustration, the aircraft remained—until word arrived that another convoy was nearing Malta.

An RAF Baltimore bomber takes off from one of Malta's airfields for a

preventive strike at enemy positions in nearby Sicily. Many veteran pilots believed that the battle of Malta was an even tougher fight than the Battle of Britain.

ACTION ON THE GIBRALTAR RUN

Wearing an antiflash hood and gloves, an officer on the British cruiser Scylla describes to shipmates belowdecks an attack on the convoy the ship is escorting.

THE BATTLE LOG
OF A CONVOY ESCORT

In the summer of 1943, the British cruiser *Scylla* took up station at Gibraltar. Her assignment: to escort Mediterranean-bound convoys along the perilous Iberian coast, the shortest route from England to Malta and North Africa. As the convoys hugged the shores of Spain and Portugal, they came within striking distance of the Germans' long-range bombers based near Bordeaux. RAF air cover was sparse at best and only heavily armed ships like the *Scylla* stood between the enemy and the defenseless merchantmen.

On board the cruiser that summer was Heywood Magee, a photographer who had joined the ship hoping to record action at sea. He was not disappointed. One day in July, the *Scylla* and her convoy came under fierce air attack. Magee was ready. His photographs on these pages document the ensuing battle, as well as daily life on board a warship.

As the *Scylla* raced from Gibraltar to meet the convoy, which was already en route to Spain's Cape Finisterre, her crew began to gird for battle: They changed from tropical kit (white shorts and shirts) to coveralls, antiflash headgear and steel helmets. The ship went on "second degree of readiness," with every sailor at his post around the clock.

Toward dusk one evening, the *Scylla's* crew saw the convoy on the horizon. "A fantastic assortment of ships, transports and once-famous liners," marveled Magee, "keeping station with Liberty ships, oil tankers, tank carriers and a wonderful mob of ocean tramps, brazen in their determination to hang closely to the sterns of the tall aristocrats. Spread out in front are the escorting destroyers, sloops and frigates of the protective screen."

As the *Scylla* joined the screen, Magee noted a subtle change in the crew's mood. "They sense battle pretty surely," he recalled. "Looking around, I see the big guns moving and the gunners getting the feel of their weapons."

The following day, when a formation of German planes appeared, the crew—all veterans of the bloody "Bomb Alley" run to North Africa in 1942—was ready. "Well, shipmates, the party is about to begin," said the torpedo officer cheerfully. "We hope to give them a very hearty reception."

Captain Ian Macintyre (right), a veteran of many escort missions, discusses convoy defense with his executive officer, Commander B. J. Fisher.

Her foamy wake stretching off to the horizon, the Scylla races to meet her convoy off Cape Finisterre, 500 miles north of the Naval base at Gibraltar.

From a wing of the bridge, a young lookout diligently scans the skies through high-powered binoculars for a glimpse of approaching German aircraft

At his action station inside one of the cruiser's turrets, a Royal Marine gunner tries to get a few hours of sleep on a cot next to an ammunition locker

Peering intently through a specially tinted filter, a lookout attempts to track a pair of Focke-Wulf bombers (right) diving at the Scylla out of the sun.

A stick of German bombs kicks up a geyser of water near the Scylla. "Time and again," observed photographer Magee, "our big guns upset their bomb aimers."

"BOMBERS APPROACHING FROM STARBOARD"

At noon on the day after the *Scylla* joined the convoy, the summer calm was shattered by a terse announcement over the ship's loudspeakers: "Focke-Wulf bombers approaching convoy from starboard." Within moments, three waves of seven planes each came snarling over the ships.

As the Focke-Wulfs started their bombing runs, the *Scylla* began stitching the sky with antiaircraft fire. One plane was able to dive through the flak barrage to drop a bomb between the *Scylla* and a freighter, showering shell fragments on the cruiser's deck. The rest of the bombers retreated.

One of the fleeing German planes was hounded by an American B-24 Liberator that was in the area by chance. The *Scylla's* torpedo officer gave a blow-by-blow account of the ensuing duel to the crew belowdecks, reporting excitedly: "The Lib is right on his tail; now he's above him. Hold on a moment, chaps, something's going to happen. It has. Jerry's plunged into the drink."

The first round had gone to the Allies, but the fight was by no means over.

Captain Macintyre barks orders from the bridge. The captain, Magee noted, was "completely at ease."

In the Scylla's fire-control center, radar operators track incoming German aircraft that are within a 20-mile radius of the ship.

A young stoker, his hand cupped over one ear to muffle the sound of the Scylla's guns, receives orders over an intercom.

Stokers regulate the four boilers amid what Magee called "a brain-racking tangle of machinery" that could propel the cruiser at a top speed of 33 knots

WHERE "YOU LEARN WHAT IT IS TO BE AFRAID"

When a new wave of Luftwaffe bombers pounced on the convoy, Magee went belowdecks, where most members of the Scylla's crew toiled at dirty jobs in claustrophobic quarters. In the torrid heat of boiler and engine rooms, far away from any glimpse of sky or sea and with only the pounding thud of the ship's guns and the torpedo officer's running description to keep them apprised of the fighting above, stokers strained to keep the cruiser's boilers perking; engineers cursed and cajoled

to get every ounce of power from the Scylla's turbines.

"We're no bloody glamor boys," a begrimed stoker told Magee. "When you've seen fine, big ships vanish in a cloud o smoke and flames within a few seconds you learn what it is to be afraid, especially when you work below.

"That's when you begin to do your job perfectly," the stoker continued. "You realize that a bomb or a tin fish gives no second chances."

GETTING EVEN WITH GUNFIRE AND CURSES

Throughout the long summer twilight, the Focke-Wulfs kept up the attack—and the *Scylla's* antiaircraft guns responded with bursting shells. "As the planes came in, we methodically placed our black blotches in straight lines across the heavens, constantly harrying the great black birds," said gunnery officer Robert Hughes.

"With grunts and curses," Hughes said, "we would watch a vicious burst rock a plane so its wings canted, and it would drop in a great curve out of danger. Time and time again accurate fire would upset their aim and the bombs would either miss or the planes would break off the attack to make a run-in from another direction."

Taking advantage of the last light before they turned back toward France, the Focke-Wulfs dropped their remaining payloads on the ship called Tail-End Charlie, traditionally the last ship in the convoy. Miraculously, the tramp steamer managed to zig and zag out of harm's way. The battle was over.

On deck, the gunnery officer tracks the paths of incoming aircraft.

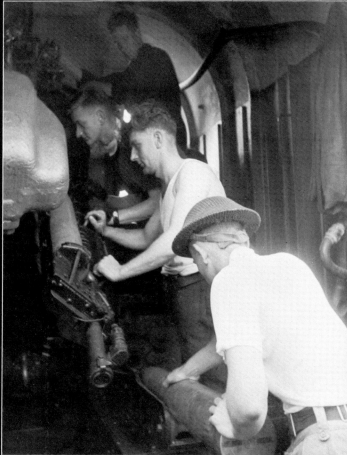

Gunners pass ammo; a skilled crew could fire up to 16 rounds per minute.

A torpedo suspended from a parachute (circled) falls toward a freighter. The Scylla's gunners were able to blow up the device before it hit the water.

The Scylla, scuppers littered with shell cases, shepherds her charges toward Gibraltar.

TAKING QUIET STOCK AFTER THE BATTLE

"The action fades away," wrote photographer Magee, "and the cease-fire sounds." Throughout the Scylla, weary crewmen took stock: After four hours of battle and thousands of rounds fired, not one ship in the convoy had been hit by an enemy bomb, not one man had been injured.

It had been a bravura performance by the Scylla—one that drew effusive praise from an American commander whose vessel was in the convoy. "Boy! Could that ship chuck shells in the air," he told all comers while celebrating his safe arrival in Gibraltar. "When that baby went out, way in front of the convoy, she was just one great sheet of flame. The Heinies never got near when she was around."

In the comfort of his cabin, Captain Macintyre (right) dictates his battle report. Such accounts usually downplayed the most dramatic action with dry prose.

5

Morning, August 11, 1942: The Mediterranean was calm and the weather balmy. Off the coast of Algeria the skipper of the *U-73*, Lieutenant Helmut Rosenbaum, listened to the thump of approaching propellers. He rotated his periscope above the water's surface and saw a submariner's dream— a convoy escorted by what he described as "a giant matchbox floating on a pond." It was a double-funneled aircraft carrier zigzagging in a series of almost right-angle turns at a speed he estimated at 12 knots. The *U-73* dived to 100 feet and threaded a path between the carrier's escorting destroyers. The eerie pinging of the asdic set resounded within the submarine. Rosenbaum sent his periscope through the surface again and again, manueuvering for the kill. At 1:15 p.m. the carrier was dead ahead: range, 500 yards. He gave the order to fire and a spread of four torpedoes slammed into the ship's port side. Eight minutes later the H.M.S. *Eagle* went to the bottom, taking 260 British crewmen to their graves with her.

Thus the Axis opened a ferocious campaign to destroy the most important Allied convoy to sail the Mediterranean during World War II. Code-named *Pedestal,* the convoy represented a do-or-die effort to relieve the tiny island outpost of Malta, which remained blockaded and besieged, its people facing starvation.

The grim situation at Malta reflected British fortunes throughout the Mediterranean in that gloomy summer of 1942. The British Navy in the Mediterranean had been reduced almost to impotence. In the desert, Rommel was preparing to launch a final assault against the cities of Alexandria and Cairo.

Malta's last hope was the *Pedestal* convoy. It had to succeed; accordingly it became the most formidable naval force ever to run the deadly gantlet to the island fortress. At its heart were 14 supply ships crammed with foodstuffs, ammunition and gasoline. Largest of the 14 was the tanker *Ohio,* on charter from the Texas Oil Company to the British Ministry of War Transport and manned by British sailors. Loaded with 11,500 tons of desperately needed kerosene and fuel oil, the *Ohio* was a floating bomb.

To protect the convoy, the Admiralty assigned a powerful flotilla of warships: the battleships *Nelson* and *Rodney,* the carriers *Indomitable, Victorious* and *Eagle,* seven cruisers and 24 destroyers. The main elements of this enormous

THE ULTIMATE CONVOY

convoy sailed from England in the early days of August 1942. And as the ships filed through the Strait of Gibraltar, Axis coastwatchers tracked their progress and plans were made to intercept them.

The forces assembled by the Axis to stop *Pedestal* were equally formidable: From Crete and North Africa, 200 Luftwaffe planes flew into airfields on Sicily and Sardinia to join the 400 Italian planes already waiting there; 21 Italian and German submarines sped to stations off the Moroccan, Algerian and Tunisian coasts. The submarines concentrated at the segment of the route where the convoy would be most vulnerable, the Sicilian Narrows, a passage 95 miles wide between Sicily and North Africa. Here, to avoid the huge shoals of the Skerki Bank southwest of Sicily, the convoy would have to skirt Tunisia's Cape Bon. Axis planes and ships turned the sea there into a minefield, and 23 motor-torpedo boats took up stations at the southeastern exit of the pass, to lie in wait. Moreover, *Pedestal* would have to negotiate the Narrows stripped of a major portion of its armor. The convoy's battleships and carriers, because they would have too little room to maneuver under fire, were under orders to turn back to Gibraltar rather than risk the constricting passage.

By August 10, when the last of the *Pedestal* ships had steamed through the Strait of Gibraltar, the Axis interceptors were deployed and waiting. It was the following day when the Germans drew first blood by sinking the *Eagle*. Barely had the shock of the carrier's loss subsided when the commander of *Pedestal*, Vice Admiral Neville Syfret, received a radio message warning of new danger: INTERCEPTED ENEMY WIRELESS TRAFFIC INDICATES THAT AIRCRAFT MAY ATTACK CONVOY AT DUSK.

At sunset, when torpedo-launching Heinkel-111s and Junkers-88s swooped down from the east, Syfret's ships were ready. Antiaircraft gunners on board the ships threw up a deadly screen of steel and explosives; at least four German planes crashed into the sea and darkness soon sent the others home. During the night the Luftwaffe stayed away while the convoy, in four columns, steamed eastward. By dawn the ships were only 70 miles from Sardinia and its Axis airfields. The antiaircraft gunners were at their stations, anticipating the attack that was sure to come. And with the first light a dozen fighter planes roared off the flight deck of the *Indomitable* to guard the supply ships.

A wave of 19 Ju-88 bombers struck at 9:15 a.m. The carrier planes met the attackers 25 miles away from the convoy, and in a swirling air battle over the sea, shot down six Junkers. A few German pilots got through, but they dropped their bombs wide of their targets.

The convoy skippers enjoyed a brief respite. Then, at noon, the Italian Air Force and the Luftwaffe staged a massive strike: nearly 140 planes in a carefully orchestrated attack of two waves. The first wave—10 Savoia torpedo planes and eight Caproni fighter-bombers, escorted by 14 Macchi fighters—introduced a new weapon to the Mediterranean war. It was the *motobomba,* a torpedo dropped by parachute and set to run in circles to disrupt the fleet. But the convoy skippers, most of whom had sailed together from England, were not easily addled. On order, they executed a coordinated 90-degree turn to starboard, leaving the *motobombas* harmlessly chasing one another's wakes. This smooth maneuver also threw off the second wave of 62 Savoia torpedo bombers. Not one managed a hit.

The Italians had another surprise for the *Pedestal* convoy—a pilotless Savoia-79 bomber, radio-controlled from another plane. It droned through a fierce antiaircraft barrage, but once over the convoy, failed to release its bomb. The Savoia flew on toward the North African coast and crashed in Algeria. Later in the day an Italian fighter-bomber pilot scored a bull's-eye on the flight deck of the *Victorious* just as she was landing her Hurricane fighters. Luckily for the *Victorious'* crewmen, the bomb was a dud.

No sooner had the Italian planes departed than 37 German dive bombers arrived to challenge the convoy's outer defenses. The 11 that made it through concentrated on the merchant ship *Deucalion,* a well-scarred veteran of previous Malta convoys. One bomb holed the *Deucalion's* deck without exploding, but near misses damaged the ship's engines. The destroyer *Bramham* fell back to escort the crippled freighter to the Tunisian coast. Darkness had almost hidden the *Deucalion* when two hostile torpedo planes came in low over the water. A torpedo hit the ship's hull and ignited her cargo of fuel. Most of the *Deucalion's* crew scrambled into lifeboats and pulled away just before their ship became a floating inferno. Other members of the crew jumped into the sea and were picked up by the *Bramham*.

At 4:16 p.m. the destroyer *Pathfinder* detected a submarine in the convoy's path and immediately attacked with depth charges. Twenty minutes later the Italian submarine *Cobalto* broke the surface near the destroyer *Ithuriel*. Her forward guns ablaze, the *Ithuriel* rammed the stricken submarine and scooped up the Italian survivors. But the destroyer's bow was crumpled by the impact, and she had to limp back to Gibraltar.

At 6:30 p.m. a combined force of German and Italian aircraft from Sicily appeared over the convoy, and while Italian torpedo planes were attacking the convoy's flanks, German Stukas dived from ahead and behind. A torpedo blew

the stern off the destroyer *Foresight* and she was scuttled the following day. Stukas buckled the *Indomitable's* flight deck with three bombs, effectively putting the carrier out of action. Her planes had to land on the nearby *Victorious*.

The convoy was approaching the most dangerous leg of the voyage, the Sicilian Narrows. This was the point at which the battleships and carriers were to retire. Admiral Syfret ordered the warships to turn back to Gibraltar under his command. The merchantmen, 12 destroyers and four cruisers, now commanded by Rear Admiral Harold Burrough, narrowed their formation from four columns to two and went on toward the Narrows.

The convoy skippers had no illusions about what awaited them in the channel. Lookouts scanned the calm sea for the needle of a submarine periscope or its feathery, telltale wake. Sonar operators huddled over their instruments, listening for the submerged enemy.

In spite of all these precautions one Italian submarine, the *Axum*, closed in undetected. At 7:27 p.m., as darkness approached, Lieutenant Renato Ferrini, the *Axum's* commander, carefully poked his periscope out of the water for a look. There they were: "About 15 steamers," Ferrini noted in his log, "two cruisers and numerous destroyers." A perfectly massed target. Ferrini maneuvered into firing position.

Fifteen minutes later he took another quick look. About a mile ahead of him were two warships and a merchantman—dead in his sights. Diving again, Ferrini moved closer. At 7:55 p.m. he fired a spread of four torpedoes, then let the *Axum* settle as he listened for the explosions. The first one rumbled back through the water in 63 seconds; 27 seconds later, two more explosions told Ferrini that three of his torpedoes had found targets.

But he could observe only by sound, for in less than five minutes, he recorded, "the hunt began with a pattern of depth charges." Ferrini dived below 300 feet and cut his engine. For two hours he was under attack—a succession of thumping depth charges, then silence, then more concussions whenever he tried to ascend.

By 10:30 p.m. the attacks had ceased. Ferrini made a gingerly reconnaissance, surfacing at a distance. The sky was lit with flames so bright that they illuminated his submarine. Ferrini had time to count three vessels afire before he no-

Rear Admiral Harold Burrough (left), escort commander of the convoy code-named Pedestal during the most perilous leg of its voyage to Malta in August of 1942, confers with Captain Harold Drew, skipper of the cruiser Manchester. In defending the convoy, Admiral Burrough's flagship was crippled and Captain Drew's ship was sunk.

The Royal Navy aircraft carriers Victorious (foreground), Indomitable and Eagle escort the Pedestal convoy eastward from Gibraltar. Like other carrier planes protecting the convoy, the Sea Hurricane and biwinged Albacore on the Victorious' flight deck had bright yellow leading wing edges and tail fins for quick identification by friendly antiaircraft gunners.

ticed two destroyers signaling each other and turning toward him. Again the *Axum* plunged beneath the surface and skittered away.

The *Axum* had claimed some rich prizes. One of her torpedoes had slammed into the port side of the escort flagship, the cruiser *Nigeria*. Electricity on board the cruiser failed as the ship listed violently to starboard. Admiral Burrough, the escort commander, leaned over the bridge railing to encourage his men on the deck below. ''Don't worry,'' he told them, ''she'll hold. Let's have a cigarette.'' The de-

stroyer *Ashanti* came alongside shortly afterward to remove the flag officer and his staff. The damaged *Nigeria* was then escorted back to Gibraltar.

Another of the *Axum's* torpedoes had struck the cruiser *Cairo*. As the *Cairo* began settling in the water, her crew abandoned ship.

The *Axum's* third torpedo had found the big tanker *Ohio*. The *Ohio's* captain, Dudley Mason, at 39 one of the youngest civilian skippers assigned to the Ministry of Transport, was on the bridge when the *Nigeria* and the *Cairo* were hit.

His third mate shouted, "Hold on to your hats; if there's another torpedo in that salvo we've. . . ." The exclamation ended in midsentence as the *Axum's* torpedo rammed into the *Ohio's* port side amidships, blowing a hole 24 feet wide in her hull. Mason gave orders to shut down the engines—and to get the fires caused by the explosion under control before they spread to the volatile cargo and turned the ship into a funeral pyre.

The attack on the *Ohio* created pandemonium in the convoy. The merchantman *Empire Hope,* steaming directly aft of the *Ohio,* had to hastily reverse its engines to avoid plowing into the stricken tanker. As the orderly formation broke up, all the other ships tried to avoid collisions by swinging aside in the narrow channel. Destroyers raced at all angles through the dark to pick up survivors and to depth-charge the submarines that now were slipping in and out of the convoy's path. To complete the chaos, the sky was suddenly filled with the sound of a rare nighttime air attack: Ju-88 bombers and Savoias swooping low to send their torpedoes slicing into the floundering convoy.

The *Empire Hope* was hit by the bombers and her cargo of aviation fuel exploded in a mighty blast. Two more merchantmen, the *Clan Ferguson* and the *Brisbane Star,* were caught by torpedoes. The *Clan Ferguson* blew up; the *Brisbane Star* was stopped dead in the water. The cruiser *Kenya* took a torpedo in her side, halted momentarily and then rushed back into the melee. Not until midnight did the planes wing away and the submarines flee before the darting destroyers.

In the eerie aftermath, the escort vessels scooped up the swimming sailors by the light of the burning ships and herded those merchant ships that were still seaworthy into a rag-

Survivors of the torpedoed aircraft carrier Eagle prepare to scramble from their lifeboats onto a rescuing destroyer 550 miles west of Malta. Some 900 of the 1,160-man crew on board the Eagle were saved.

ged column. The fires on board the *Ohio* had been extinguished. The destroyer *Ledbury* came alongside the tanker to offer a tow. "No, thank you," Captain Mason called back from the bridge, "we are under our own steam, but we haven't got a compass. Can you lead us to the convoy?"

The *Ledbury* did so, but gave Mason a scare on the way by heading for water that was aflame with gasoline discharged from a sunken ship. Mason, trying to follow behind, seized his megaphone. "For God's sake keep clear of that," he shouted. "We're oozing paraffin!"

As the crippled convoy limped past Cape Bon, it moved directly into yet another ambush. Lurking in the darkness and hidden by a headland of the Tunisian coast were the 23 German and Italian motor-torpedo boats. The swift little craft rolled gently on the calm sea, their engines stilled, waiting for their prey to come within optimal range. Then they roared to life.

At 1 a.m. the attack boats swept down on the crippled convoy. A torpedo rammed into the cruiser *Manchester*, flooding her engine room and fouling her steering gear. The ship lost all power, and when it became apparent that she could not be saved her crew scuttled her, took to the lifeboats and set off for the Tunisian coast. The merchantmen *Wairangi, Glenorchy* and *Almeria Lykes* went to the bottom with torpedo holes in their hulls. The *Rochester Castle*, weaving in evasive action, took a torpedo in her forward hull. Her watertight compartments held and she wallowed on. Not so fortunate was the merchant ship *Santa Elisa*, which came under attack simultaneously from port and starboard, confusing her gunners. A torpedo penetrated her hull, igniting her gasoline cargo; her crew scrambled overboard just before the ammunition in her hold exploded.

The onslaught continued through the night; not until dawn did the torpedo boats go away. First light revealed a stricken convoy. Of the 14 original supply ships, only six were still afloat. Struggling to keep up with the others was the tanker *Ohio*. The crew had managed to shore up her bulkheads, but the weakened hull plates were throbbing as she pushed along at 16 knots.

As the broken formation steamed on that morning, Admiral Burrough pondered an ominous message he had received. A reconnaissance plane had signaled that the Italian Navy was coming out after *Pedestal*. The pilot had sighted six cruisers and 11 destroyers in the Tyrrhenian Sea, headed on a course that would intercept the convoy south of Pantelleria Island, still 200 miles from Malta. A force that large could blow the rest of *Pedestal* out of the water, for Burrough at this point had only two cruisers and seven destroyers in his command.

At this crucial point, the Italians hesitated. The commanders, wary of the Allied planes at Malta and gripped by vivid recollections of the British triumph at Taranto, demanded German air cover for their fleet. But the Luftwaffe, having tasted the convoy's blood, insisted on using all its planes in a last assault to destroy the damaged survivors before they could reach Malta. The dispute reached all the way to Mussolini; he decided in favor of the Germans.

The Italian commanders were further deterred by an RAF ruse. Pilots from Malta kept their radios buzzing with details of a huge squadron of planes taking off to attack the Italian fleet. It was fiction, but it worked. The Italian ships veered north and returned to their home ports. In a humiliating final touch, the British submarine *Unbroken*, prowling north of Sicily, torpedoed the retreating cruisers *Bolzano* and *Attendolo*, putting both out of action for the duration of the War.

Spared from the Italian surface fleet, the *Pedestal* convoy still faced an all-out challenge from combined Italian and German air forces. The first wave, a dozen Ju-88s, swept down from the north at 8 a.m. on August 13. The merchant ship *Waimarama*'s cargo of high-octane aviation fuel was ignited by a bomb and erupted into a giant fireball. So great was the explosion that sheets of steel plate and piping from the *Waimarama* rained down on the trailing merchant ship *Melbourne Star*, which had to rudder hard to avoid colliding with the burning hulk. The *Ohio* also bore perilously close to the *Waimarama*. "Hard a-port! For God's sake, hard a-port!" Captain Mason bellowed to his first officer. Both ships narrowly escaped the *Waimarama*'s flames.

Then, at 9:25 a.m., 60 Stukas and Italian fighters swept in from Sicily and singled out the *Ohio*. The Axis aircraft dived on the tanker from all directions, churning the sea with spouts of white water, but they failed to score a hit. A damaged Stuka plunged Kamakazi-style onto the *Ohio*'s deck, showering aircraft parts over the ship. Its bomb failed to detonate. The *Ohio*'s luck was holding, but it was running thin.

Ju-88s dropped parachute mines and torpedoes in the *Ohio's* path. The tanker eluded them. Two 550-pound bombs straddled her hull; Chief Engineer James Wyld in the engine room swore later that his ship had left the water and become airborne. The *Ohio's* electricity failed, and her boilers died. Her crew relighted the boilers and brought the tanker's speed back to 16 knots, but shock waves from more near misses delivered what seemed to be the *coup de grâce.* A large puff of black smoke escaped from the *Ohio's* bullet-ridden stack, and her engines went dead. "It's all over, lad, I'm afraid," Wyld told a sailor. "In five minutes we won't have steam to steer her."

Although the *Ohio* had lost her engines, she was still afloat. If she could be towed to Malta, 70 miles away, her precious cargo could still be saved. The destroyer *Penn* came alongside to pass a towline to her, but while the two ships were dead in the water more dive bombers struck, hitting the tanker amidships at the waterline. The *Ohio* began to settle. Mason ordered the crew to abandon ship.

But, amazingly, the tanker still floated. A minesweeper, the *Rye,* and two motor launches arrived on the scene from Malta to help with the tow, and a call went out for volunteers to board the crippled tanker. Captain Mason became indignant: "Volunteers be damned!" he growled. "We've still got a crew, haven't we?" The *Ohio's* crewmen returned to their ship.

The vessels from Malta joined the *Penn* in a new attempt to tow the *Ohio.* Just as the tanker started to move, a bomb struck near her stern and a second crashed into her engine room and exploded. Again, it looked as if the *Ohio* would go under. Her crew was taken off once more and the ship was left, listing and settling, to her fate.

During the night of August 13, the *Penn* and the *Rye* tied up to the wallowing hulk and managed to get her moving again. Mason and some of his crew members went back on board. The towlines broke. They made them fast again. The destroyers *Bramham* and *Ledbury* joined in the effort. While the rest of the convoy went on ahead, the towing vessels, engines pounding, struggled to get the *Ohio* to Malta before she sank. For a day and a half they nursed the sinking giant along, and on the morning of August 15 they nudged the tanker into Valletta harbor. On the shore, thousands of Maltese cheered their arrival.

Waiting in the inner harbor were *Pedestal's* four other surviving merchant ships: the *Port Chalmers,* the *Rochester Castle,* the *Melbourne Star* and the *Brisbane Star.* The *Ohio* was gingerly moored beside two auxiliary tankers, and Mason eyed her battered hull. "It isn't over yet," he cautioned. "This poor old hooker hasn't got many minutes now. I hope to God she lasts long enough." She did, but barely; soon after her fuel was discharged to the auxiliary ships, the *Ohio* slowly settled to the harbor floor.

The cost of Operation *Pedestal* had been fearsome: nine merchantmen and four Naval ships sunk, three more warships severely damaged and some 350 sailors lost. Malta had been resupplied, however—and it was now evident that without the assistance of a surface navy, Axis submarines and airplanes could not stop a determined, well-escorted convoy in the Mediterranean.

So long as the Italian fleet avoided battle, Luftwaffe commanders would make no further attempt to contest Malta-bound convoys. The island's supply problem gradually ended. Grand Harbor once again bustled with activity; Maltese airfields buzzed with RAF planes. Soon after Operation *Pedestal,* Allied shipping lanes in the southern Medi-

Burning aviation fuel sends up a column of greasy black smoke from the British merchant ship Waimarama, struck by Luftwaffe dive bombers 170 miles northwest of Malta.

YANK SUPPORT FOR THE RAF

Britain's beleaguered forces in the Mediterranean received some unexpected help in the summer of 1942. A flight of 13 American B-24s touched down in Egypt in June; they were assigned to execute but a single mission—bombing the oil fields of Rumania. The British, who were in desperate need of long-range, heavy bombers, promptly persuaded Washington to leave the unit in Egypt.

In their first outing, in support of a convoy bound for Malta, the B-24s scored hits on Italian warships and shot down a German fighter—the first kill by American planes in the Middle East. The airmen later racked up impressive scores against Axis strongholds in North Africa, Greece and Crete, stretching what was to have been a brief sojourn into a fruitful campaign.

Harry Halverson (right), who led the B-24 unit, with General Elmer Adler.

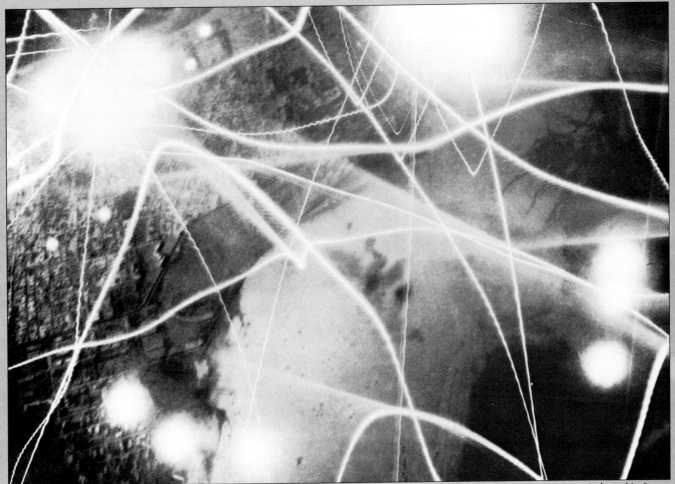

German antiaircraft fire illuminates the sky over the Libyan port Benghazi during a bombing raid in 1942 by American B-24s based in Egypt.

terranean opened up and it was no longer necessary to supply the British Army in Egypt by convoys sent around Africa and through the Suez Canal. But control of these ship routes was only the first step in securing the Mediterranean. The Axis powers could still strike at Mediterranean targets from their airfields in southern Europe. The Afrika Korps held substantial territory in Libya and Tunisia. And Hitler still had the power to send troops into southern France and Spain, thereby bottling up the western Mediterranean.

The question that had most divided Allied strategists during the spring and summer of 1942 had been whether to relegate the Mediterranean to secondary status and fight the War in western Europe, or to secure North Africa, with its ports and airfields, then plunge northward through what Churchill optimistically referred to as Europe's "soft underbelly." Once the decision was made to invade North Africa first, the Allies poured their combined resources into an ambitious operation that Churchill personally code-named *Torch*. An American, Lieut. General Dwight D. Eisenhower, was selected to lead the Allied Expeditionary Force. (Ironically, Eisenhower, whose skill had yet to be tested on a battlefield, was one of those who had steadfastly opposed the North Africa venture.) Britain's Admiral Cunningham, because of his long experience in the Mediterranean, was named deputy commander.

Most of the troops and many of the ships in the invasion

force would be American. On October 25, 1942, ports on the East Coast of the United States were alive with activity as battleships, cruisers, destroyers, troop transports and hundreds of support vessels—from tankers to tugs—weighed anchor and headed across the Atlantic. That same day the American aircraft carrier *Ranger* and four escort carriers sailed from Bermuda, taking precautions to avoid U-boats by describing what an admiral called "the track of a reeling drunk in the snow." Three days later the carriers joined the armada: nine columns of warships and merchantmen that covered a 500-square-mile patch of ocean. This convoy, which was designated the Western Naval Task Force, was assigned to land 35,000 combat troops, 250 tanks and support equipment on three separate Moroccan beaches, north and south of Casablanca.

While the American fleet was steaming eastward, two additional invasion convoys—the Center and Eastern Naval Task Forces—set sail from the United Kingdom. The first convoy carried 39,000 American troops destined for beaches near Oran and the second 23,000 British and 10,000 American troops assigned to land near Algiers. Tactical plans called for the three convoys to coordinate their arrivals in the landing zones so that their amphibious forces would hit the beaches simultaneously.

As the armadas converged on North Africa, General Eisenhower, Admiral Cunningham and a small staff went to Gibraltar to set up the command post for the operation, now scheduled to begin on Sunday, November 8. It had already been delayed when the body of an Allied naval officer, whose plane was shot down off the Spanish coast, washed up near Cádiz; in his pockets were top-secret letters with details of the invasion. Allied agents were able to get to the body before any Axis spy or sympathizer could, but the incident caused an anguished postponement.

Gibraltar was not the ideal location for a command post, but it was the only safe Allied-held vantage point near the invasion beaches. Eisenhower and Cunningham established themselves in dank offices deep inside the echoing caverns of the Rock. It was, Eisenhower recalled, "the most dismal setting we occupied during the War." Dark tunnels cut through the solid limestone were lit by a few bare light bulbs. The air was stale, and water dripped from the ceiling. The only communication with the oncoming invasion fleet

Lord John Gort, the British Governor of Malta, sets a fuel-conservation example by bicycling through the city of Valletta. Such gestures endeared Gort to the embattled islanders, who called him "Malta's luck."

was by weak radio signals, which kept fading out. Reports competed with rumors. (One rumor had it that German agents in Spain were keeping track of Allied ships passing through the Strait of Gibraltar by using sensors to detect the heat from their funnels.)

But there was solid news from Egypt. Rommel's Afrika Korps had begun retreating from El Alamein with Montgomery's Eighth Army in hot pursuit. Mussolini would be denied his triumphal ride through Cairo. On the 6th of November, General Sir Harold Alexander, Commander in Chief of Allied forces in the Middle East, cabled London: "Ring out the bells," and nearly every church tower in England resounded joyously.

In Gibraltar that evening, Cunningham emerged from his warren, climbed the headland at Europa Point and peered across the dark waters to the south. Beyond the harbor, jammed gunwale-to-gunwale with tugs and tankers, he could see the blacked-out ships of the invasion fleet, silently steaming eastward toward Oran and Algiers.

Almost immediately, the Algiers-bound convoy came under attack. Thirty-three miles east of the Cape of Palos, Spain, a German U-boat slammed a torpedo into the American transport Thomas Stone, carrying 1,400 assault troops of the 39th Infantry Regiment. The troopship wallowed to a stop. To slow the convoy and transfer the Thomas Stone's human cargo to other ships would delay the landing schedule. But to abandon the transport would almost ensure a second attack. The ship's commanding officer, Captain Olten R. Bennehoff, and a senior infantry officer aboard, Major Walter Oakes, quickly improvised a solution. They disembarked 800 soldiers into 24 of the ship's most seaworthy landing craft and dispatched them in three ragged columns toward the Bay of Algiers, some 150 miles away. The Thomas Stone herself was taken in tow.

The solution soon ran into trouble. The shallow-draft, flat-bottomed landing craft had not been designed for a long haul in the open sea. Their engines quickly overheated and their oil lines burst. When one boat broke down the entire flotilla stopped to wait while repairs were made. Waves washed over the gunwales and the unprotected troops became wet, cold and seasick. After one miserable night of this, it was obvious that the unusual armada would never be able to make it to the North African shore. Men and equipment were crowded aboard an escorting British corvette, the Spey, and the landing craft were scuttled. The troops reached Algiers 24 hours late.

Trouble of a different sort threatened the western task force approaching Casablanca. The Atlantic weather had turned foul; seas were heavy and the surf was running 15 feet high. The landing craft would never survive such conditions. General Eisenhower's staff seriously considered diverting the task force into the Mediterranean for a landing in calmer waters. But at the last possible moment the task force commander, Rear Admiral H. Kent Hewitt, forwarded

A Maltese boy, his pet dog on a leash, unfurls a Union Jack in the rubble-strewn streets of Valletta to celebrate the arrival of a convoy.

his weathermen's prediction that the storm would pass in time for the landings. Eisenhower decided to go ahead as planned, setting a pattern he would consistently follow whenever bad weather endangered invasion forces under his command.

The weather was not the only cause for concern. Morocco and Algeria were French territories; despite months of secret negotiations with pro-Allied French officials, no one in the Allied camp knew whether the French would fight back, or how hard. Churchill had put the problem succinctly: "The first victory we have to win is to avoid a battle; the second, if we cannot avoid it, to win it." President Roosevelt had recorded a radio message for broadcast by the BBC to the French in North Africa. The message promised that the Allies had no territorial aspirations and needed French soil only to continue the fight against the Axis. Eisenhower, in a subsequent broadcast, asked Vichy officials to switch on coastal searchlights and train them overhead as a friendly signal. Although the broadcasts were repeated each half-hour, few Frenchmen heard them, and the night before the landings the skies over Casablanca, Oran and Algiers were illuminated only by defensive searchlights picking out Allied ships and planes operating offshore.

The question of French reaction was answered sharply in preliminary commando operations just before the main landings on November 8. The Allied plan called for three destroyer squadrons to disembark antisabotage raiding parties in the inner harbors of Oran and Algiers and in the harbor of Safi, Morocco.

When the U.S. destroyers *Cole* and *Bernadou* steamed past the jetty protecting Safi harbor just before dawn, they were met at almost point-blank range with heavy machine-gun, 75mm and 155mm artillery fire. The American invaders took special care not to be mistaken for the British, whom the French defenders—vividly remembering the Royal Navy's attack on the French fleet at Mers-el-Kebir—held in particular disdain.

The *Bernadou* signaled her identity by sending up a flare from which an illuminated American flag floated down by parachute, but the French answered by lighting up the harbor with star flares and intensifying their gunfire. Rear Admiral Lyal Davidson, commander of an attack group in the

Spread across the calm waters of the Atlantic, a massive invasion fleet steams eastward from the United States in November of 1942 for the invasion of North Africa. Two other convoys carrying Anglo-American forces were sailing simultaneously from ports in Great Britain.

task force, gave the order for his men to return the fire (his signal was coded in an imperative familiar to baseball fans: "Play Ball"). Shortly afterward, guns on the cruiser *Philadelphia* and the battleship *New York* opened up against the shore batteries. In the meantime, the *Bernadou's* crewmen commenced firing with large- and small-bore weapons. The destroyer nudged the shore and her 197 raiders clambered down nets to the rocks, where they quickly organized an attack on defending French Legionnaires.

Despite machine-gun fire from shore, the destroyer *Cole* managed to tie up at the commercial pier. Her troops, along with those from the *Bernadou*, rapidly subdued French strong points and took control of the port. The Allies had their first foothold.

In their tunnel headquarters on Gibraltar, Eisenhower and Cunningham monitored radio reports throughout the night and listened to the *drip-drip* of water from the ceiling ticking off the minutes before H-hour. At Oran and Algiers, French resistance had stopped the other two raiding parties in their tracks. But just before dawn the Allied commanders knew that virtually every ship of their main forces was on station, the landing craft were heading for shore—and the weather was moderating on the Atlantic beaches. Nevertheless, Cunningham was fretful. The main landings were a major—and complicated—gamble. Few of the British and none of the Americans in the three amphibious groups had ever seen action. On the American cruiser *Brooklyn*, for example, only nine of the 65 officers had been in the Navy more than three years, and more than half of the enlisted men were at sea for the first time.

Cunningham's fears were soon confirmed. The landings in Morocco were chaotic from the start. Some landing craft were overloaded, and shipped enough water to drown their engines. Others collided in the choppy seas. Many more were beached on rocks. At Fédala, 15 miles north of Casablanca, all but seven of the 25 landing craft in the first wave from the transport *Charles Carroll* were wrecked; five of the surviving craft were lost returning to the beaches in a second wave. The transport *Wood* sent in 32 boats for the initial landing but only 11 returned. It was even worse on the Mediterranean beaches; overall the loss of landing craft approached 40 per cent.

The transfer of supplies from ship to shore was just as poorly executed. Inexperienced crews often dumped equipment pell-mell on the beaches and headed back to the transports for another load. A supply report read: "It was as though some gigantic overhead scoop full of supplies had suddenly emptied its contents. Apparently nothing had been hauled away and nothing had been stacked." A quartermaster's list for one pile of stores left on a Moroccan beach included three sections of steel matting, a case of wienerwurst, two 10-gallon field containers of aviation fuel, some pistol ammunition, lubricating oil, a cluster of 105mm artillery shells and a case of strawberry jam.

Had the French mounted a more widespread defense at the water's edge, the confusion that characterized the Allied landings might have doomed Operation *Torch*. But some of the Vichy troops were ambivalent about firing on the Allied landing parties; as a consequence, resistance was sporadic. By November 10, two days after the first landings, the combination of Allied guns and sustained diplomatic pressure had persuaded the French in North Africa to lay down their arms.

Word of the capitulation moved Hitler to retaliate at once: He activated a contingency plan for the German occupation of the Vichy-controlled zone of France, and by nightfall German tanks and troops were on the move. The take-over shattered any hopes the French government may have had of preserving its neutrality. Admiral Darlan immediately ordered the French fleet in Toulon—a still-potent force of 77 warships—to set sail for North Africa. The move was easier ordered than executed. Luftwaffe planes mined the entrance to the harbor at Toulon and packs of German U-boats prowled the approaches. Moreover, the French Naval commanders suffered divided loyalties and in the critical days when escape to North Africa was still feasible, they lost valuable time squabbling.

Hitler suffered from no such indecision; he had no intention of allowing the French ships to join the Allies. Early on November 27 two German armored columns rolled through Toulon to take possession of the port and the fleet, which still had not moved. Forewarned of the Germans' approach, Admiral Jean de Laborde, Commander in Chief of the High Seas Fleet, took the desperate action that he considered commensurate with French national honor. He radioed his ship captains: SCUTTLE! SCUTTLE! SCUTTLE! French sailors ruefully raced against the clock to destroy their ships before the Germans arrived.

In the predawn hours German tanks smashed through the harbor's outer perimeter but got lost amid the labyrinth of docks and sheds. Then, in perhaps the most incongruous duel of World War II, a German Tiger tank rolled onto Milhaud pier, firing its 88mm gun at the battle cruiser *Strasbourg*, a survivor of the British attack on Mers-el-Kebir. The *Strasbourg* could not lower its 13-inch turret guns to pier level to demolish the pesky tank, but French machine gunners on deck opened fire at the intruder. A German shell slammed into one of the *Strasbourg's* turrets, killing the lieutenant in charge and wounding six crewmen. Eventually Admiral de Laborde ordered his men to cease firing.

The Germans were too late anyway. The scuttlers had done their work; explosive charges began detonating inside gun after gun. Hand grenades exploded in vital machinery. Water flooded through open sea cocks and the *Strasbourg* began to settle to the harbor floor.

Other French crews were following the same proud but painful course. When a German officer reached the pier beside the cruiser *Algérie*, he informed Vice Admiral Émile Lacroix, "We have come to take over your ship."

"You are a little late," the Admiral retorted. "It is already sinking."

"Will it blow up?"

"No."

"In that case," replied the German officer, "we will go aboard."

"In that case," said Lacroix, "it will blow up."

All told, the French had destroyed one battleship, two battle cruisers, seven cruisers, 32 destroyers, 16 submarines and 19 smaller vessels. Their denial to the Germans eliminated one of Hitler's last chances to prevail in the Mediterranean. Only one Axis fleet remained to challenge Allied domination—the Italian warships that, since their buffeting at Taranto, had avoided offensive action.

The Italian Navy soon would be tested again. Allied strategists already were discussing an invasion of the Italian homeland. Italy would enjoy a respite only as long as the Allies were occupied in North Africa. The quick victories in the coastal cities at the outset of Operation *Torch* had proved deceptive, and it would take another six months for Eisenhower's forces to fight their way eastward and squeeze the Axis armies between themselves and Montgomery, who was heading west. But in January of 1943, with the desert campaign at last flowing in the Allies' favor, Churchill and Roosevelt and their combined staffs gathered at Casablanca to decide where to strike next in the Mediterranean. The choice was Sicily.

Capturing the island off the toe of the Italian boot would remove a source of persistent Axis attacks on the nearby Mediterranean supply routes, and once taken it would provide an excellent staging area for an invasion of the mainland. The operation was code-named *Husky*, with Eisenhower at its head and Cunningham as its naval commander.

The North Africa invasion had been history's largest amphibious operation; the initial assault on Sicily was to be even larger: 80,000 Allied troops, 600 tanks, 7,000 trucks and other vehicles, and 900 guns to be transported in 3,300 ships and boats of every available type, brought from as far away as the United States. The movements of this vast fleet would have to be orchestrated into scores of convoys, all plotted precisely to converge on a crowded shoreline, through waters that were within easy range of Axis bombers, torpedo planes and submarines—and, if it chose to fight, the Italian surface fleet. If anything went wrong with this enormously complicated first step, the question of tactics ashore would become academic.

And there was a more immediate problem. D-day for *Husky* had been set for early July. But the Axis forces in North Africa were still holding out, tying up Allied troops and equipment essential for the Sicily adventure. Not until May 12 and 13 did the Axis forces, trapped on the Cape Bon peninsula, lay down their arms. General Alexander radioed London: WE ARE MASTERS OF THE NORTH AFRICAN SHORES. Allied commanders in the Mediterranean were now free to concentrate fully on the Sicily landings less than two months away.

Cunningham moved to Malta on July 4 and set up a headquarters for the invasion. The island lay in ruins from years of relentless air bombardment. The imperturbable Maltese had come out of their air-raid-shelter caves and were rebuilding their homes. They paused to cheer A.B.C. and his

ATTEMPTS TO SALVAGE A SCUTTLED FLEET

Admiral Jean de Laborde's orders to scuttle the French fleet stressed that the ships must not be capsized, in the hope they might one day sail again for France. As a result, most of the 77 ships that fell into German hands in November 1942 rested on fairly even keels in the shallows of Toulon harbor. But it was Italian engineers who first tried to salvage them. Some of the vessels, including the cruisers *Colbert* (opposite) and *Algérie,* were so severely damaged they had to be scrapped. But in nine months of intense effort, the Italians refloated or dry-docked 30 of the craft.

To the dismay of the French, the Italians then confiscated what they had salvaged. The aircraft catapult and thick turret armor of the battle cruiser *Strasbourg* were removed and shipped to Italy along with the

superstructure and interior fittings of the battle cruiser *Dunkerque.* From the smaller cruisers, the salvagers took just about everything left above the waterline. Seven destroyers and a submarine—the vessels least damaged—were taken to Italian waters, either in tow or under their own steam. But these vessels soon changed flags again: When Italy surrendered, the Germans reconfiscated them.

The Germans returned control of the partly salvaged wrecks that remained in Toulon to France. But with small crews that included neither antiaircraft gunners nor fire fighters, the vessels made easy targets for Allied bombs. Six were resunk in a single raid in November 1943. By August 1944, when the Allies landed near Toulon, none of the salvaged ships were afloat.

Admiral Jean de Laborde, the French commander in Toulon who gave the order to scuttle, hoped his fleet would rise again.

Oil smoke from the burning French fleet in Toulon harbor silhouettes the battle cruiser Strasbourg, which has settled with her main deck still above water.

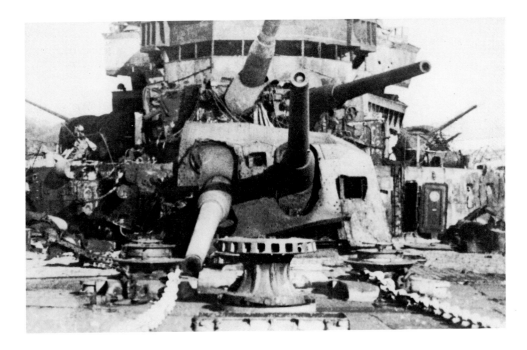

Explosions on board the cruiser Colbert just as German troops reached her deck left the barrels of her 8-inch forward guns wildly askew. The ship was beyond reclamation.

A lone German soldier stands guard in Toulon over scuttled French patrol vessels, whose flags hang forlornly from the halyards.

staff as he moved back into Admiralty House. Eisenhower arrived four days later, and he and Cunningham settled into a command post in the Lascaris tunnel, carved out of Malta's sandstone. There was no dripping water here; the Lascaris tunnel was arid, stifling, stinking and infested with sand flies. Their bites infected some of the staff officers with sand-fly fever, retarding the staff operation.

D-day for *Husky* was July 10, H-hour 2:45 a.m. And on

the morning of July 9, as the invasion transports were assembling off Malta, the weather turned nasty. A mistral, the harsh gale dreaded by all Mediterranean sailors, came shrieking down from the northwest. By afternoon the winds had risen to more than 30 miles per hour. Even the largest ships were taking green water over their bows. Assault troops, crammed into poorly ventilated compartments, became seasick. The plunging and wallowing vessels nearly

Italian Admiral Alberto da Zara (right) salutes a Royal Navy honor guard as he ceremoniously surrenders a squadron of warships to the British at Malta. Above, 16 Italian submarines lie interned at Sliema harbor on the northeastern coast of Malta shortly after Italy's capitulation.

collided as their helmsmen struggled to control them. The open landing craft became sloshing tubs; the soldiers huddled in them were drenched.

On Malta, Eisenhower spent much of the afternoon in Cunningham's office monitoring weather reports. As with the North Africa landings eight months earlier, the meteorologists predicted that the storm might quickly blow itself out. Cunningham, the old Mediterranean hand, recalled that blows like this often died down at dusk. Eisenhower decided to gamble: There would be no postponement.

Cunningham went to the harbor to watch the Malta contingent leave for Sicily. He watched the ships "literally burying themselves, with the spray flying over them in solid sheets, as they plunged out to sea on their way to their assault positions." His anxieties, Cunningham recalled, "were not at all relieved." Later that afternoon the admiral and his chief of staff drove to an airfield "for want of something definite to do. It was the last place we should have visited. All the winds of heaven seemed to be roaring and howling round the control tower. We returned to Admiralty House in deep anxiety."

Darkness came, and the heavy wind continued. Cunningham rode out to Delimara Point to see if he could spot the troop-carrying gliders heading for Sicily. Standing on the promontory, he saw the gliders and their towplanes sweep over at 300 to 400 feet, their dim navigation lights flickering in the sky. The gale nearly drowned out the towplane engines. "In the pale half-light of the moon they looked like flights of great bats," he recalled. But he noticed that the wind was finally moderating.

Back in the operations room the chart had become a crosshatch of lines indicating the Allied fleet, which was blacked out and under radio silence, converging on Sicily. After midnight Cunningham and Eisenhower, without undressing, climbed into their bunks for a couple of hours of restless sleep.

During the night Vice Admiral Hewitt of the U.S. Navy had assembled 580 ships, transporting 1,124 shipborne landing craft. To the east his British counterpart, Vice Admiral Sir Bertram Ramsay, had marshaled 795 ships with 715 landing craft. To guard against intervention by the Italian fleet, based at the mainland ports of La Spezia and Taranto, a Royal Navy task force of battleships, carri-

ers, cruisers and destroyers operated boldly off the east coast of Sicily. This task force also had a secondary objective—to feign a major amphibious landing in Greece in conjunction with false information that British Intelligence had leaked to the Germans.

Cunningham was up before H-hour, waiting for a report from his ships. It came at 5 a.m. The first group of Royal Marine Commandos was safely ashore. He rushed to Eisenhower's office. Ike was up, and other messages were soon pouring in. The landings were successful all along the targeted coast. The defenders evidently had decided that on such a wild night at sea nobody would attempt an amphibious operation. And the Italian Navy never left port.

Sicily fell to the Allies in 38 days. The Axis forces resisted all the way, fighting short, sharp rear-guard actions, then retreated to the mainland. In a masterfully organized evacuation, 40,000 Germans and 70,000 Italians, with most of their equipment, were ferried across the narrow Strait of Messina to Italy and temporary haven.

The Allies were close behind them. On September 3, Allied forces began to cross the Strait of Messina, setting the stage for landings later that month at Taranto and Salerno, farther up the Italian boot. By the 8th of September, Italy had had enough of the War and surrendered. Germany was left, without its once-powerful partner, to fight the Allies on two fronts.

The day after Italy's surrender, a contingent of the Italian Navy steamed out of Taranto and crossed paths with a British squadron bringing reinforcements to Italy. For a few minutes British gunners manned their weapons, their commanders watching tensely. But the Italian fleet proceeded peacefully to internment at Malta.

The following day at Grand Harbor, Admiral Cunningham witnessed what he called "a most moving and thrilling sight": his former flagship, the *Warspite*, "which had struck the first blow against the Italians three years before, leading her erstwhile opponents into captivity." And on the 11th of September, 1943, he sent a jubilant message to the Lords of the Admiralty in London: "Be pleased to inform their Lordships that the Italian battle fleet now lies at anchor under the guns of the fortress of Malta." The Mediterranean once more was "Cunningham's Pond."

A SEA WAR COMMEMORATED

The Royal Navy light cruiser Manchester (left) and the battleship Rodney beat back Axis air attacks on the Pedestal convoy, steaming for Malta.

PROFILE OF A CAMPAIGN WITHOUT MONUMENTS

The French battleship Provence (left) is flanked by British warships in Alexandria in 1940. The British later shelled the Provence at Mers-el-Kebir.

On the warm spring night of May 3, 1943, the sea off the Tunisian coast was rent by a cataclysmic explosion. An Italian transport carrying an enormous cargo of artillery shells, bombs and land mines had been blown up by gunfire from three patrolling British destroyers. The thunderclap signaled the end of the battle for control of Mediterranean shipping lanes, the central drama of a three-year campaign. Italy's merchant fleet was now virtually extinct, and no more of its transports would brave the ''death route'' southward past the British stronghold of Malta to North Africa. By contrast, Allied convoys were steaming to Malta and Alexandria almost unopposed.

For both sides, the toll had been terrible. Wrote a British veteran: ''Rusting off every cape and headland, and disintegrating beneath the blue acres of the sea, lay millions of tons of merchant and naval shipping, together with the whitening bones of men from almost every race under the sun.''

Though the Mediterranean war had seen some spectacular naval actions near Cape Matapan and Italy's Calabrian shores, the critical contests had been fought by submarines and aircraft operating off Sicily, Malta and the Axis-held African coast. Lieut. Commander Malcolm D. Wanklyn's submarine *Upholder* alone had sunk 128,353 tons of Axis shipping and claimed the lives of thousands of German and Italian soldiers before being sunk herself. Indeed, submarines had turned out to be Britain's strongest weapon in the Mediterranean. ''More than any other single arm,'' wrote Admiral Sir Andrew Cunningham, ''they played a decisive part in cutting the Axis supply lines to Libya, helping to make possible the eventual advance of the Eighth Army to Tripoli and beyond.''

No monuments mark the sites of the battle of Matapan, the surprise British air attack on Taranto or the last resting place of the *Upholder* and her crew. But the events and the fighting men are commemorated in a series of paintings by artist David Cobb, a reserve officer stationed at Gibraltar. Commissioned by the Royal Navy, they are published for the first time on these pages.

British warships based at Gibraltar steam past the Rock. Ships operating from Gibraltar could strike into the Atlantic or into the western Mediterranean.

The most famous of the British U-class submarines, the Malta-based Upholder, attacks an Italian troopship convoy at dawn on September 18, 1941. By autumn of 1942, the Upholder and other British undersea raiders were sinking nearly half the Axis shipping sent to North Africa.

Braving heavy antiaircraft fire, one of 21 Swordfish from the aircraft carrier Illustrious launches its torpedo against the Italian fleet at Taranto. The British sank or disabled three battleships and lost only two planes.

Led by the battleship Littorio, an Italian fleet turns away from a Malta-bound convoy off the coast of North Africa on the 22nd of March, 1942. Smoke screens laid by British destroyers prevented the Italians from sighting on the convoy or its outgunned escort, and the British destroyers' daring torpedo attacks finally forced the Italians to break off the action.

During the battle of Matapan, the British battleships Warspite, Valiant and Barham demolish the Italian cruisers Fiume and Zara on the night of March 28, 1941. "Our searchlights shone out with the first salvo," Admiral Cunningham recalled. "The Italians were quite unprepared. They were helplessly shattered before they could put up any resistance."

A flight of Stukas attacks Malta in one of the daily raids that punished the island in the spring of 1942. The Luftwaffe almost succeeded in isolating and crushing Malta, but urgent calls for air support from German armies fighting in Libya and on the Russian front drained off the bombers, permitting the British to regain control of the air over the Mediterranean.

The carrier Illustrious bears the brunt of a concentrated dive-bombing attack by three squadrons of Stukas while on convoy duty in January 1941. The Illustrious sustained six direct hits by 1,000-pound bombs; she survived them thanks to her armored flight deck and her crew's superb damage-control work.

The aircraft carrier Eagle, torpedoed by the German submarine
U-73 as she set out to accompany the Pedestal convoy, lists to port before
sinking with a loss of 260 lives. In addition to escorting nine British
convoys, the veteran ship earlier had ferried 183 fighter planes to Malta.

The tanker Ohio, lashed between two other ships, is towed into Malta
harbor at the completion of the Pedestal voyage. Torpedoed, struck
by bombs, set on fire, twice abandoned and reboarded, dead in the water
and sinking, the Ohio survived her ordeal to deliver 10,000 tons of fuel
for the island's cooking stoves, dock machinery, planes and submarines.

BIBLIOGRAPHY

Adams, Henry H., *Years of Deadly Peril*. David McKay, 1969.

Angelucci, Enzo, and Paolo Matricardi, *World War II Airplanes*, Vol. 1. Rand McNally, 1976.

Ansel, Walter, *Hitler and the Middle Sea*. Duke University Press, 1972.

Auphan, Paul, and Jacques Mordal, *The French Navy in World War II*. Transl. by A. C. J. Sabalot. United States Naval Institute, 1959.

Badoglio, Pietro, *Italy in the Second World War*. Transl. by Muriel Currey. Greenwood Press, 1976.

Bekker, Cajus, *The Luftwaffe War Diaries*. Transl. and ed. by Frank Ziegler. London: Macdonald & Co., 1966.

Belden, Jack, "Malta Wins the Siege." *Life*, February 15, 1943.

Bernotti, Romeo, *La Guerra sui Mari nel Conflitto Mondiale, 1939-1941*. Livorno, Italy: Società Editrice Tirrena, 1950.

Borghese, J. Valerio, *Sea Devils*. Transl. by James Cleugh. London: Andrew Melrose, 1953.

Boutron, Eric, *De Mers-el-Kébir à Londres, 1940-1944*. Paris: Éditions Plon, 1980.

Bradford, Ernle, *Mediterranean: Portrait of a Sea*. Harcourt Brace Jovanovich, 1971.

Bragadin, Marc' Antonio:
The Italian Navy in World War II. Transl. by Gale Hoffman. United States Naval Institute, 1957.
"Mediterranean Convoys in World War II." *Proceedings*, U.S. Naval Institute, February 1950.

Brown, David:
Carrier Fighters: 1939-1945. London: Macdonald and Jane's, 1975.
Carrier Operations in World War II, Vol. 1, *The Royal Navy*. Naval Institute Press, 1974.

Brown, Eric:
Wings of the Navy: Flying Allied Carrier Aircraft of World War II. London: Jane's Publishing, 1980.
Wings on My Sleeve. Shrewsbury, England: Airlife Publications, 1978.

Bryant, Arthur, *The Turn of the Tide*. Doubleday, 1957.

Buckley, Christopher, *Greece and Crete: 1941*. London: Her Majesty's Stationery Office, 1977.

Butcher, Harry C., *My Three Years with Eisenhower*. Simon and Schuster, 1946.

Cameron, Ian:
Red Duster, White Ensign. Doubleday, 1960.
Wings of the Morning: The British Fleet Air Arm in World War II. William Morrow, 1963.

Campbell, Christy, ed., *Naval Aircraft*. Chartwell Books, 1977.

Cantel, Rudy, *L'Attentat de Mers-el-Kébir*. Paris: La Technique du Livre, 1943.

Chatterton, E. Keble, *Britain at War*, Vol. 3, *The Royal Navy: From April 1942 to June 1943*. London: Hutchinson & Co., no date.

Churchill, Winston S., *The Second World War*:
Vol. 1, *The Gathering Storm*. Houghton Mifflin, 1948.
Vol. 2, *Their Finest Hour*. Houghton Mifflin, 1949.
Vol. 3, *The Grand Alliance*. Houghton Mifflin, 1950.
Vol. 4, *The Hinge of Fate*. Houghton Mifflin, 1950.
Vol. 5, *Closing the Ring*. Houghton Mifflin, 1951.

Ciano, Galeazzo, *Ciano's Hidden Diary: 1937-1938*. Transl. by Andreas Mayor. E. P. Dutton, 1953.

Cocchia, Aldo, *The Hunters and the Hunted*. Transl. by M. Gwyer. United States Naval Institute, 1958.

Collier, Richard, *Duce! A Biography of Benito Mussolini*. Viking Press, 1971.

Cooper, Bryan, *PT Boats*. Ballantine Books, 1970.

Craven, Wesley Frank, and James Lea Cate, *The Army Air Forces in World War II*:
Vol. 2, *Europe: Torch to Pointblank, August 1942 to December 1943*. The University of Chicago Press, 1949.
Vol. 7, *Services around the World*. The University of Chicago Press, 1958.

Cunningham of Hyndhope, Viscount:
"Report of an Action with the Italian Fleet off Calabria, 9th July, 1940." Supplement to *The London Gazette*, April 27 and 28, 1948.
A Sailor's Odyssey. London: Hutchinson & Co., 1951.

Davies, John, *Lower Deck*. Macmillan, 1945.

De Belot, Raymond:
"The French Fleet in Being." *Proceedings*, U.S. Naval Institute, October 1951.
The Struggle for the Mediterranean: 1939-1945. Transl. by James A. Field Jr. Princeton University Press, 1951.

De la Penne, Luigi Durand, "The Italian Attack on the Alexandria Naval Base." *Proceedings*, U.S. Naval Institute, February 1956.

Dönitz, Karl, *Memoirs: Ten Years and Twenty Days*. Transl. by R. H. Stevens. Greenwood Press, 1976.

Edwards, Kenneth, *Men of Action*. London: Collins, 1943.

Eisenhower, Dwight D., *Crusade in Europe*. Doubleday, 1948.

Farrar-Hockley, Anthony, *Student*. Ballantine Books, 1973.

Feis, Herbert, *Churchill, Roosevelt, Stalin*. Princeton University Press, 1957.

Fermi, Laura, *Mussolini*. The University of Chicago Press, 1961.

Fest, Joachim, *Hitler*. Transl. by Richard and Clara Winston. Vintage Books, 1970.

Flower, Desmond, and James Reeves, eds., *The Taste of Courage: The War, 1939-1945*. Harper & Brothers, 1960.

Fraccaroli, A., *Italian Warships of World War II*. London: Ian Allen, 1968.

Gibson, Hugh, ed., *The Ciano Diaries: 1939-1943*. Doubleday, 1946.

Gleason, James, and Tom Waldron, *Midget Submarine*. Ballantine Books, 1975.

Gwyer, J. M. A., and J. R. M. Butler, *Grand Strategy*, Vol. 3, *June 1941-August 1942*. London: Her Majesty's Stationery Office, 1964.

Hanson, Norman, *Carrier Pilot*. Cambridge, England: Patrick Stephens, 1979.

Hart, Sydney, *Submarine Upholder*. London: Oldbourne Press, 1960.

Hay, Ian, *Malta Epic*. D. Appleton-Century, 1943.

Hibbert, Christopher, *Benito Mussolini: A Biography*. London: The Reprint Society, 1962.

Hitler, Adolf:
Hitler's Secret Book. Transl. by Salvator Attanasio. Grove Press, 1961.
Hitler's Secret Conversations: 1941-1944. Transl. by Norman Cameron and R. H. Stevens. Farrar, Straus and Young, 1953.

Hoffmann, Heinrich:
Hitler in Italien. Munich: Verlag Heinrich Hoffman, 1938.
Hitler Was My Friend. Transl. by R. H. Stevens. London: Burke, 1955.

Hogan, George, *Malta: The Triumphant Years, 1940-1943*. London: Hale, 1978.

Horsley, Terence, *Find, Fix and Strike: The Work of the Fleet Air Arm*. London: Eyre and Spottiswoode, 1943.

Hughes, Robert, *Through the Waters: A Gunnery Officer in H.M.S. Scylla, 1942-1943*. London: William Kimber, 1956.

Hurd, Sir Archibald, *Britannia Has Wings!* London: Hutchinson & Co., 1942.

Ireland, Bernard, *The Aircraft Carrier: An Illustrated History*. Chartwell Books, 1979.

Kemp, P. K.:
History of the Royal Navy. G. P. Putnam's Sons, 1969.
Victory at Sea: 1939-1945. London: Frederick Muller, 1957.

Kesselring, Albert, *Kesselring: A Soldier's Record*. William Morrow, 1954.

Kirkpatrick, Ivone, *Mussolini: A Study in Power*. Hawthorn Books, 1964.

Lamb, Charles, *War in a Stringbag*. London: Arrow Books, 1977.

Langer, William L., and S. Everett Gleason, *The Undeclared War: 1940-1941*. Peter Smith, 1968.

Langmaid, Rowland, "The Med": The Royal Navy in the Mediterranean, 1939-45. London: The Batchworth Press, 1948.

Lash, Joseph P., *Roosevelt and Churchill: 1939-1941, the Partnership That Saved the West*. W. W. Norton, 1976.

Leighton, Richard M., and Robert W. Coakley, *United States Army in World War II: The War Department, Global Logistics and Strategy, 1940-1943*. Office of the Chief of Military History, Department of the Army, 1955.

Lewis, Peter, *The British Bomber since 1914: Fifty Years of Design and Development*. Aero Publishers, 1967.

Linklater, Eric, *The Second World War, 1939-1945: The Campaign in Italy*. London: Her Majesty's Stationery Office, 1951.

Lipscomb, F. W., *The British Submarine*. London: Conway Maritime Press, 1975.

Lloyd, Sir Hugh, *Briefed to Attack: Malta's Part in African Victory*. London: Hodder & Stoughton, 1949.

Macintyre, Donald:
Aircraft Carrier: The Majestic Weapon. Ballantine Books, 1968.
The Battle for the Mediterranean. W. W. Norton, 1975.
Fighting Admiral: The Life of Admiral of the Fleet Sir James Somerville. London: Evans Brothers, 1961.
Wings of Neptune: The Story of Naval Aviation. W. W. Norton, 1963.

Magee, J. H., "Into Action: Aboard a Cruiser." *Picture Post* magazine, Vol. 20, No. 11, September 11, 1943.

Mars, Alastair:
British Submarines at War: 1939-1945. Naval Institute Press, 1971.
Unbroken: The Story of a Submarine. London: Frederick Muller, 1953.

Martienssen, Anthony, *Hitler and His Admirals*. E. P. Dutton, 1949.

Mason, David, *Who's Who in World War II*. Little, Brown, 1978.

McMillan, Richard, *Mediterranean Assignment*. Doubleday, Doran, 1943.

Middlebrook, Martin, and Patrick Mahoney, *Battleship: The Loss of the Prince of Wales and the Repulse*. London: Allan Lane, 1977.

Moore, John, *The Fleet Air Arm: A Short Account of Its History and Achievements*. London: Chapman & Hall, 1943.

Moorehead, Alan, *Mediterranean Front*. McGraw-Hill, 1942.

Morison, Samuel Eliot, *History of United States Naval Operations in World War II*:
Vol. 2, *Operations in North African Waters, October 1942-June 1943*. Little, Brown, 1975.
Vol. 9, *Sicily-Salerno-Anzio, January 1943-June 1944*. Little, Brown, 1975.

Moss, W. Stanley, *Ill Met by Moonlight*. London: George G. Harrap, 1950.

Murphy, Robert, *Diplomat among Warriors*. Greenwood Press, 1964.

Newton, Don, and A. Cecil Hampshire, *Taranto*. London: William Kimber, 1959.

Oliver, Leslie, *Malta at Bay*. London: Hutchinson & Co., 1942.

Pack, S. W. C.:
Cunningham the Commander. London: B. T. Batsford, 1974.
Operation "Husky": The Allied Invasion of Sicily. Hippocrene Books, 1977.
Sea Battles in Close-up, Vol. 2, *Night Action off Cape Matapan*. United States Naval Institute, 1972.

Playfair, I. S. O., *The Mediterranean and Middle East*:
Vol. 1, *The Early Successes against Italy (to May 1941)*. London: Her Majesty's Stationery Office, 1954.
Vol. 2, "The Germans Come to the Help of Their Ally" (1941). London: Her Majesty's Stationery Office, 1956.
Vol. 3, *British Fortunes Reach Their Lowest Ebb (September 1941 to September 1942)*. London: Her Majesty's Stationery Office, 1960.
Vol. 4, *The Destruction of the Axis Forces in Africa*. London: Her Majesty's Stationery Office, 1966.

Polmar, Norman, *Aircraft Carriers: A Graphic History of Carrier Aviation and Its Influence on World Events*. Doubleday, 1969.

Ramsay, Winston G., ed., "Gibraltar." *After the Battle* magazine, No. 21.

London: Battle of Britain Prints, 1978.

Rich, Norman, *Hitler's War Aims: The Establishment of the New Order*. W. W. Norton, 1974.

Roskill, S. W., *H.M.S. Warspite*. London: Collins, 1957.

Roskill, S. W., *The War at Sea, 1939-1945*:
  Vol. 1, *The Defensive*. London: Her Majesty's Stationery Office, 1954.
  Vol. 2, *The Period of Balance*. London: Her Majesty's Stationery Office, 1956.
  Vol. 3, *The Offensive*. Parts 1 and 2. London: Her Majesty's Stationery Office, 1961.

Roskill, Stephen, *Churchill and the Admirals*. William Morrow, 1978.

Schofield, B. B., *Sea Battles in Close-up*, Vol. 6, *The Attack on Taranto*, Naval Institute Press, 1973.

Seth, Ronald, *Two Fleets Surprised: The Story of the Battle of Cape Matapan, Mediterranean, March 1941*. London: Geoffrey Bles, 1960.

Shankland, Peter, and Anthony Hunter, *Malta Convoy*. Ives Washburn, 1961.

Sherwood, Robert E., *Roosevelt and Hopkins: An Intimate History*. Harper & Row, 1950.

Showell, J. P. Mallmann, *U-boats under the Swastika: An Introduction to German Submarines, 1935-1945*. Arco Publishing, 1973.

Skiera, Joseph A., ed., *Aircraft Carriers in Peace and War*. Franklin Watts, 1965.

Smith, Peter C., and Edwin Walker, *Sea Battles in Close-up*, Vol. 11, *The Battles of the Malta Striking Forces*. London: Ian Allan, 1974.

Spencer, John Hall, *Battle for Crete*. London: William Heinemann, 1962.

Stitt, George, *Under Cunningham's Command: 1940-1943*. London: George Allen & Unwin, 1944.

Taylor, J. W. R., and P. J. R. Moyes, *Pictorial History of the RAF*. Arco Publishing, 1968.

Terraine, John, *The Life and Times of Lord Mountbatten*. Holt, Rinehart and Winston, 1980.

Thetford, Owen:
  Aircraft of the Royal Air Force since 1918. London: Putnam, 1979.
  British Naval Aircraft: 1912-1958. London: Putnam, 1977.

Thomas, David A., *Crete 1941: The Battle at Sea*. London: New English Library, 1975.

Turner, John Frayn, *Periscope Patrol: The Saga of Malta Submarines*. London: George G. Harrap, 1957.

Tute, Warren, *The Deadly Stroke*. Coward, McCann & Geoghegan, 1973.

Varillon, Pierre, *Mers-el-Kébir*. Paris: Éditions Amiot-Dumont, 1949.

Vian, Sir Philip, *Action This Day: A War Memoir*. London: Frederick Muller, 1960.

Von der Porten, Edward P., *The German Navy in World War II*. Galahad Books, 1969.

Warner, Oliver, *Admiral of the Fleet, Cunningham of Hyndhope: The Battle for the Mediterranean*. The Ohio University Press, 1967.

Werner, Herbert A., *Iron Coffins: A Personal Account of the German U-boat Battles of World War II*. Holt, Rinehart and Winston, 1969.

Wilmot, Chester, *The Struggle for Europe*. Harper & Row, 1963.

PICTURE CREDITS

Credits from left to right are separated by semicolons, from top to bottom by dashes.

COVER and page 1: Ullstein Bilderdienst, Berlin (West). 2, 3: Map by Tarijy Elsab.

HITLER'S MOMENTOUS VISIT—8, 9: Hugo Jaeger, *Life*, © Time Inc. 10: From *Hitler in Italien* by Heinrich Hoffmann, © 1938, published by Verlag Heinrich Hoffmann, Munich. 11: Hugo Jaeger, © Time Inc. 12: Popperfoto, London—Süddeutscher Verlag, Bilderdienst, Munich. 13, 14: Hugo Jaeger, © Time Inc. 15: From *Hitler in Italien* by Heinrich Hoffmann, © 1938, published by Verlag Heinrich Hoffmann, Munich. 16, 17: Hugo Jaeger, © Time Inc.; Süddeutscher Verlag, Bilderdienst, Munich—Stato Maggiore della Marina, Rome. 18, 19: From *Hitler in Italien* by Heinrich Hoffmann, © 1938, published by Verlag Heinrich Hoffmann, Munich; Hugo Jaeger, © Time Inc.

ROILING "CUNNINGHAM'S POND"—22: Imperial War Museum, London. 23: Ullstein Bilderdienst, Berlin (West). 24: Thomas McAvoy for *Life*. 25: Courtesy Commander Marc' Antonio Bragadin, Rome. 26, 27: Charles E. Brown from Pictures Inc. 28: Wide World. 30, 31: UPI. 32: Jean-Loup Charmet, courtesy Musée des Deux Guerres Mondiales, Paris.

CARNAGE AT MERS-EL-KEBIR—34, 35: E.C.P. Armées, Paris. 36: Imperial War Museum, London; Photo Bibliothèque Nationale, Paris. 37: Imperial War Museum, courtesy Archives Tallandier, Paris. 38, 39: Musée de la Marine, Paris—E.C.P. Armées, Paris. 40, 41: E.C.P. Armées, Paris; UPI. 42, 43: Popperfoto, London. 44, 45: Photo Bulloz, courtesy Musée de la Marine, Paris; UPI.

BRITAIN'S INVALUABLE ROCK—46, 47: Wide World. 48: Map by Tarijy Elsab. 49: Imperial War Museum, London. 50, 51: Keystone Press, London; Imperial War Museum, London. 52, 53: Imperial War Museum, London. 54, 55: Imperial War Museum, London (2); Popperfoto, London. 56, 57: Imperial War Museum, London (2); Dever from Black Star. 58, 59: Imperial War Museum, London.

LIGHTNING STRIKE AT TARANTO—62: Publifoto Notizie, Milan. 65: Art by John Batchelor, London. 66, 67: RAF Museum, Hendon, England; Art by John Batchelor, London. 68: Imperial War Museum, London. 69: Courtesy Commander Marc' Antonio Bragadin, Rome. 70, 71: Art by John Batchelor, London. 73: Farabola, Milan. 74: Vice Admiral Giuseppe Fioravanzo, courtesy Ufficio Storico, Stato Maggiore della Marina, Rome, from *United States Naval Institute Proceedings*, January 1956, Vol. 82, No. 1.

AIRFIELDS AFLOAT—76, 77: Fox Photos Ltd., London. 78: Imperial War Museum, London—Keystone Press, London. 79-87: Imperial War Museum, London.

RETREAT BY SEA—90: Ullstein Bilderdienst, Berlin (West). 91: Museo Aeronautico Caproni di Taliedo, Rome. 93: From *Briefed to Attack: Malta's Part in African Victory*, by Air Marshal Sir Hugh Lloyd, © 1949, published by Hodder and Stoughton, London. 94: Jack Keates for *Life*. 96: Map by Tarijy Elsab. 98: Pictures Inc. 99: Imperial War Museum, London. 101: Keystone Press, London—Walter B. Lane for *Life*.

AID FOR A FALTERING ALLY—104, 105: Bundesarchiv, Koblenz. 106: ADN-Zentralbild, Berlin, DDR. 107: Collection of Karl-Wilhelm Grützemacher, Munich. 108: ADN-Zentralbild, Berlin, DDR. 109: Imperial War Museum, London—National Archives No. 306-NT-505IV. 110, 111: Bundesarchiv, Koblenz (2); Imperial War Museum, London. 112, 113: Bundesarchiv, Koblenz; Süddeutscher Verlag, Bilderdienst, Munich. 114, 115: Bundesarchiv, Koblenz; Collection of Karl-Wilhelm Grützemacher, Munich.

A SPECIAL KIND OF NAVY—116, 117: Stato Maggiore della Marina, Rome. 118: Courtesy Commander Marc' Antonio Bragadin, Rome. 119: Heirs of Valerio Borghese, Rome. 120: Courtesy Commander Marc' Antonio Bragadin, Rome (2)—Stato Maggiore della Marina, Rome. 121: Arrigo Barilli, Bologna. 122, 123: Roma's Press, Rome; Wide World. 124: Stato Maggiore della Marina, Rome. 125: Courtesy Commander Marc' Antonio Bragadin, Rome. 126: National Maritime Museum, London (2); Imperial War Museum, London—J. Clarkson, Preston, England—Tyne and Wear County Council, England—National Maritime Museum, London. 127: National Maritime Museum, London—R. J. Scott—National Maritime Museum, London—Skyfotos Ltd., Kent, England; National Maritime Museum, London (4). 128, 129: Stato Maggiore della Marina, Rome.

"SHOCK AFTER SHOCK"—132: Imperial War Museum, London. 134: The Illustrated London News Picture Library, London. 135: Collection of Karl-Wilhelm Grützemacher, Munich. 137: Stato Maggiore della Marina, Rome (2)—Lino Pellegrini, Milan. 139: Courtesy Commander Aldo Fraccaroli, Lugano, Switzerland. 141: Courtesy Admiral Luigi Durand de la Penne, Genoa; Stato Maggiore della Marina, Rome. 142: Imperial War Museum, London. 143: Ullstein Bilderdienst, Berlin (West). 144: Imperial War Museum, London.

THE UNQUENCHABLE MALTESE—146-151: Imperial War Museum, London. 152, 153: Imperial War Museum, London, except top left, The Illustrated London News Picture Library, London. 154, 155: National Archives No. 208-AA-228UU-1; The Illustrated London News Picture Library, London (2). 156, 157: The Illustrated London News Picture Library, London; Imperial War Museum, London.

ACTION ON THE GIBRALTAR RUN—158-171: BBC Hulton Picture Library, London.

THE ULTIMATE CONVOY—174: J. O. H. Burrough, Worcestershire, England. 175: Imperial War Museum, London. 176: Courtesy Commander Marc' Antonio Bragadin, Rome. 178: From *Malta Convoy* by Peter Shankland and Anthony Hunter, © 1961, published by David McKay Co., Inc. 179-181: Imperial War Museum, London. 182, 183: National Archives No. 80-G-40879. 186, 187: Collection Viollet, Paris; E.C.P. Armées, Paris—Photo Lapi Viollet, Paris; Ullstein Bilderdienst, Berlin (West). 188: Imperial War Museum, London.

A SEA WAR COMMEMORATED—190, 191: Derek Bayes, courtesy the artist David Cobb and The Royal Naval Museum, Portsmouth, England. 192: Artist David Cobb, Hampshire, England. 193-201: Derek Bayes, courtesy the artist David Cobb and The Royal Naval Museum, Portsmouth, England.

ACKNOWLEDGMENTS

For help given in the preparation of this book, the editors wish to express their gratitude to E. H. M. Archibald, National Maritime Museum, London; Gérard Baschet, Éditions de l'Illustration, Paris; Hans Becker, ADN-Zentralbild, Berlin, DDR; Dana Bell, Defense Audio-Visual Agency (Air Force), Arlington Still Photo Depository, Arlington, Virginia; Claude Bellarbre, Musée de la Marine, Paris; Major Peter J. Bonser, Royal Signals, Fortress Headquarters, Gibraltar; Commander Marc' Antonio Bragadin, Italian Navy (Ret.), Rome; J. D. Brown, Naval Historical Library, Ministry of Defense, London; J. O. H. Burrough, Worcestershire, England; Mary Cargill, General Reading Room Division, Library of Congress, Washington, D. C.; Jacques Chantriot, Musée de la Marine, Paris; T. C. Charman, Imperial War Museum, London; H. G. Childs, National Maritime Museum, London; G. Clout, Imperial War Museum, London; Cécile Coutin, Curator, Musée des Deux Guerres Mondiales, Paris; Hervé Cras, Former Director for Historical Studies, Musée de la Marine, Paris; Admiral Luigi Durand de la Penne, Italian Navy (Ret.), Genoa; Commander Aldo Fraccaroli, Italian Navy (Ret.), Lugano, Switzerland; Enos Garutti, Rome; Karl-Wilhelm Grützemacher, Deisenhofen, Germany; Dr. Gerhard Hümmelchen, Arbeitskreis für Wehrforschung, Stuttgart; Captain Gino Jori, Italian Navy (Ret.), Rome; Heidi Klein, Bildarchiv Preussischer Kulturbesitz, Berlin (West); Dr. Roland Klemig, Bildarchiv Preussischer Kulturbesitz, Berlin (West); Gabriel Labar, Service Historique de la Marine, Vincennes, France; David Lyon, National Maritime Museum, London; R. W. Mack, RAF Museum, Hendon, England; Admiral Massimiliano Marandino, Italian Navy (Ret.), Director, Ufficio Storico, Stato Maggiore della Marina, Rome; François Mercier, Institut d'Histoire du Temps Présent, Paris; Marjolaine Mathikine, Director for Historical Studies, Musée de la Marine, Paris; P. R. Mellor, Public Record Office, Kew, Surrey, England; Commander Nicola Morello, Italian Navy, Stato Maggiore della Marina, Rome; Luisa Mouston, Ufficio Storico, Stato Maggiore della Marina, Rome; Meinrad Nilges, Bundesarchiv, Koblenz, Germany; Dorothy Osbon, National Maritime Museum, London; Charles Pérussaux, Curator, Bibliothèque Nationale, Paris; Photographic Department, Imperial War Museum, London; Winston G. Ramsay, *After the Battle* magazine, London; Michel Rauzier, Librarian, Institut d'Histoire du Temps Présent, Paris; Nicola Scadding, Royal Naval Museum, Portsmouth, England; Commander Filippo Maria Solomone, Italian Navy, Stato Maggiore della Marina, Rome; D. S. Stonham, National Maritime Museum, London; Catherine Touny, Musée de la Marine, Paris; James H. Trimble, Archivist, National Archives, Still Photo Branch, Washington, D.C.; Colin White, Royal Naval Museum, Portsmouth, England; Marjorie Willis, BBC Hulton Picture Library, London; Cecilia Zimmermann, Barbaro, Malta. Quotations from *A Sailor's Odyssey* by Viscount Cunningham of Hyndhope. London: Hutchinson & Co., © 1951, reproduced by permission of the author.

The index for this book was prepared by Nicholas J. Anthony.

205

Printed in U.S.A.